BUILD YOUR OWN
FANTASY TREE HOUSE

BUILD YOUR OWN
FANTASY TREE HOUSE

DAVID PARFITT

METRO BOOKS
NEW YORK

This book was conceived, designed, and produced by
Ivy Press
210 High Street
Lewes
East Sussex BN7 2NS
United Kingdom

Creative Director | Peter Bridgewater
Publisher | Sophie Collins
Editorial Director | Jason Hook
Art Direction | Karl Shanahan / Wayne Blades
Designer | Wayne Blades
Project Manager | Kate Shanahan
Commissioning Editor | Libby Hayward
Photography | Simon Punter
Illustration | David Parfitt
Props | Anna Davies

Metro Books
122 Fifth Avenue
New York, NY 10011

ISBN: 978-1-4351-2719-7

Printed in China

10 9 8 7 6 5 4 3 2 1

COPYRIGHT HOLDER'S NOTE

AUTHOR'S ACKNOWLEDGMENTS

My thanks must go to Jane Sybilla Fordham for her help, throughout. To the
construction crew: Tig Evans, Alex Collins, Jane Sybilla Fordham, and Matthew
Mills. To Jane, Ivan, and Ralph Hissey for the trees, tea, and cat. To Duncan
Noël-Paton, Victoria Finnegan, and all those at Holmbush, and also to Libby
and Anna and all at Ivy who may not get a mention elsewhere.

Thanks are also due to the models who feature in the finished tree houses:
Guy and Gemma Beagley; Georgia and Romy Cooper; Aimee and Alfie Dyer;
Freya, Yelena, and Amalia Finnegan; Ralph Hissey; Dale and Lauren Hook;
Zef Howerd; and Harvey Randell.

PICTURE ACKNOWLEDGMENTS

The publishers would like to thank the following for permission to reproduce
their images: Corbis pages 6, 10, 13 (top); Getty Images pages 7, 11; The
LuEsther T. Mertz Library of The New York Botanical Garden, Bronx, New York/
engraver Stefano Della Bella page 8; and Alan Walker, page 12.

CONTENTS

Introduction

There are few practical reasons why houses should be built in trees. Unless they are sited in a rain forest or a swamp, tree houses are not practical shelters, and yet they are found in different cultures all over the world. The reason for their popularity is that tree houses are fantasy creations, and they appeal to a profound sense of excitement.

A tree house is a playful contradiction in many ways. By being neither on the ground nor in the air it dispenses with the need for foundations or wings. It is a collaboration, partly made by hand, partly by nature. From the outside it appears to be a miniature version of the world, but from within it provides an elevated view of its surroundings.

In the West, the appeal that tree houses hold is often explained as a childish thing, and it is true that given half a chance, a tree and some wood, most children will at some point make a fabulous domain all of their own. But the impulse that drives children to do this is not peculiar to them; it is universally human. To see the enjoyment of tree houses purely as a form of play is to miss the point.

TREE-HOUSE FANTASIES

Play is an activity where we engage with the improbable and the poetic—where normal rules are suspended and we can gain insights into everyday realities. Tree houses are real manifestations of these imaginary journeys, places where it is difficult to do anything but "play." Life in a tree house turns the tables to make everyday reality a temporary suspension of play. It is not surprising that adults seem to feel the contrast that tree houses offer much more than children do.

left *A rope ladder to another world holds an irresistible allure for most children.*

far left *This tree house appears to have grown organically from some accumulated driftwood. The cliff exaggerates its height and provides a dramatic, if perhaps rather short-lived, vantage point.*

7

above The amazing seventeenth-century tree house at the Villa Medici in Pratolino, near Florence, Italy. In this contemporary etching, the artist, Stefano della Bella, has managed to leave the detail up to the imagination and retain the tree house's essential mystery.

To children, they offer a familiar continuation of the world of play; to adults, a tree house may represent a return to a world that they have not visited for some time. Perhaps our insistence that tree houses fall within the child's domain recognizes the expertise that children exhibit when it comes to play. A child automatically understands that tree houses are symbolic locations for play, ideal settings for reenacting the social interaction and everyday situations that are the universal subjects of play.

When children build tree houses, they seldom have access to materials, tools and expertise, and, as a result, their tree houses tend be individual and ingenious constructions. A single plank can represent a whole wall or roof, and sometimes even the platform will be dispensed with in favor of a flag or sign. This clear focus on simple, responsive design that allows for inventive interpretation of what is important is worth remembering when a project gets oversophisticated or loses sight of its scope. In contrast, adults have better access to forms and methods of construction. There is a danger that once you are equipped with all the technology available, the simple poetry of a tree house can become lost and the tree relegated to little more than a support. However, where the technical expertise is used with sensitivity and as a way of remaining playful, especially with larger projects, it can lead to extraordinary structures that inspire all who see them. The parts that are most easily imagined are not necessarily the parts that need to be materially represented. Don't neglect the quirky detail when seeking to capture a child's imagination. Even better, involve children in the design and let them contribute as much as possible.

REFLECTIONS OF PERSONALITY

The few enigmatic histories of individual tree houses tell more about the people who built them than they do about the structures themselves. Pliny the Elder tells of the Roman emperor Gaius Caligula, who was so struck with the way a particular plane tree reminded him of a house that he had planks laid across the branches so that he could hold a reception for fifteen guests in what he called his "nest." Pliny comments that the emperor himself added to the shade it cast, presumably by his own bulk. Fabulous marble tree palaces were built by the Medici in Renaissance Florence, and it is hard to imagine these structures without wondering what size of tree could have supported them. It is no coincidence that all the historical individuals associated with tree houses were usually known for being visionaries or fantasists in some way. In literature, tree houses often appear when the author wants to emphasise an unexplored, wild land of the imagination. The tree house built by the Swiss Family Robinson is the realization of their taming the wilderness, and its building coincides with the naming of the uncharted land.

A TREE-HOUSE HANDBOOK

This is a practical book first and foremost, giving you all the information you need to make a tree house. It is for everyone interested in making something themselves to delight their friends and family. The instructions assume only basic practical ability and if you have even a basic familiarity with working wood the projects should present no difficulties. We have introduced new skills and techniques as the book progresses, alongside basic woodworking techniques for those who might need them.

In case you have grand ambitions, we have been careful not to limit the scope and ambition of the projects, but, in order to provide good learning examples, we have built them to suit young children. All the tree-house examples in this book are relatively small and close to the ground but can be used as the basis for major constructions. It is unlikely you will actually build all the projects, but it is worth reading them all for the variety of techniques and approaches that each contains.

THE PROJECTS

In this book, the projects show you how to build two different types of platform fo
each of three sites: trees with straight trunks, trees with forks, and pairs of trees. There
are then two separate themed structures for each of these six platforms. Thus, the
book presents 12 distinct tree houses, which can be adapted to fit almost any tree o
combination of trees or form the basis of your own unique designs.

Making a tree house is an opportunity
for you to use appropriate technology
but don't feel that your carpentry ha
to be of cabinetmaking quality. Where
appropriate, we have provided hints and
suggestions throughout the book, and
there are also specific sections where we
consider tools and materials; trees and
construction; the importance of safety
and design development.

None of the projects is difficult to
make, but each has an emphasis on a
different method of construction. Some
may appear complex but involve only a
few specifically shaped parts. To some
people, cutting may seem daunting
whereas using a lot of stock lumber may
not. To others, a large number of square
parts is preferable to cutting a freehand
shape. Often the success of a project i
a matter of confidence. Remember tha
there is no right way to build a tree house
Trees are not square or uniform, so each
tree house is unique. The same should
go for your construction style: make i
your own.

Building a fantasy project should be
a fun experience for everyone involved
With this book at hand, you can make the
process as enjoyable as it will be to play in
the finished tree house.

right *This indigenous tree house, built in the rain forest in Irian Jaya province in Indonesia, forms a natural part of its surroundings. Built to provide shelter, and warmth, and with an instinctive understanding of available materials, the result shows dramatic use of palm fronds and branches.*

far right *This tree house uses technology that was developed for ground dwelling, so provides instant familiarity. The placement of the platform beams works around the trees' lack of right angles.*

Practical Considerations

All the projects should be fun to make as well as to inhabit. Two things will ensure that they are enjoyable instead of frustrating to build. The first is some help from a friend or two: to hold heavy pieces while you measure, to pass things up to you while you work on the upper level of the tree house, and so on. The second is that you read all the instructions for your project (beginning with the basic platform) several times before you start. None of the tree houses is complex, but there will be fewer hitches if you understand the whole sequence of construction before you're halfway through it. So read first, then build.

below left *When is a shed not a shed? When it is up a tree. This tree house may not be useful for storing garden equipment, but it offers a place to escape to and dream.*

right *It is easy to imagine the hours of delight spent making this tree house; the process can be more important than the result.*

below right *The basics of platform and shelter make up this tree house. The choice of materials is vital when building something this simple—choose something that feels right to you.*

Every tree house should consist of six main elements:

A GOOD STRONG TREE
You may have a tree in mind. If it has suggested itself, it is probably suitable. Ensure that the tree will be strong enough to support the load, or scale down your ambitions.

GOOD ATTACHING POINTS ON THE TREE
Has the tree got features that could be used for support, such as spreading branches or a fork? Has it got clear lengths of parallel trunk for attachment points? These are crucial to the health of the tree and the stability of the tree house. Is it necessary to build high up? Even a low house can give a sense of height.

A STRONG PLATFORM SECURELY ATTACHED TO THE TREE
This is the foundation for your tree house and it must be sturdy and able to take the weight of the structure and its occupants.

A METHOD OF ACCESS
Is there a natural route up to the platform, or will you need to build a ladder or create some steps or footholds?

A PLATFORM ENCLOSURE
Should the tree house be a shelter or a sundeck? Is it a place to hide away or a stage for performing on? Whatever it's for, it must feel secure and be safe.

A COMPLEMENT TO ITS ENVIRONMENT
A successful tree house appears comfortable in its surroundings. It could merge into its background or refer to a nearby feature; or perhaps you want it to stand out? All these elements are variable and dependent on one another. To be successful, they should be balanced to create a unified construction. The projects included in this book can be starting points for designing a unique tree house for your specific needs and location.

DESIGNING YOUR OWN TREE HOUSE

below You will be amazed at the infinite variety of structures that can form the basis for your own unique tree-house design.

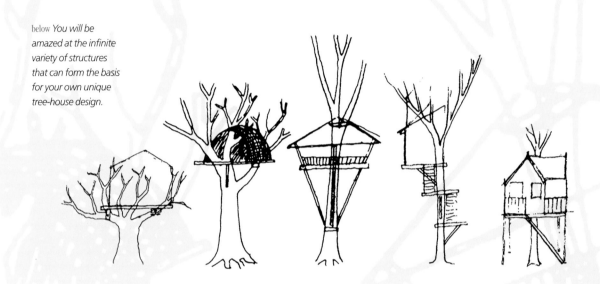

If you want to adapt any of the projects in this book, your primary concern must be the safety of the structure. The tree house must be able to withstand all the forces that will act on it. The creation of every tree house will present its own set of problems and its own unique delights. However, whatever structure you are designing and working on there are several important points you should bear in mind:

THE WEIGHT OF THE OCCUPIED STRUCTURE
You must always make sure that the entire platform is adequately supported, and you should use triangular braces wherever possible. Consider the leverage that may be exerted on any protruding parts. Decide whether to use additional wire rope for supporting weight in tension, or wooden posts or braces to prop up weight in compression.

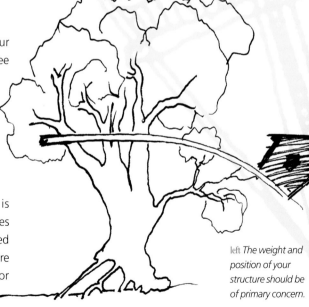

left The weight and position of your structure should be of primary concern.

14

below Trees are designed to adapt to high winds, but a tree house may not adjust to the pressure so easily.

below Unlike the tree, your tree house will need sealing to protect it from the elements.

below Consider the pressure brought to bear by the natural sway of the trees that support a tree house.

WIND

Strong winds can exert incredible pressure on a structure, so take this added stress into account when you construct your tree house. Make sure that any large surfaces, such as walls or roof panels, are securely attached to solid points, or make them easily removable in high winds.

RAIN

Rainwater will promote rot in the wood and rust in the fastenings. Be sure to protect the tree house by sealing the wood and providing good drainage and ventilation around it.

THE MOVEMENT OF THE TREE

You must always take into account that the tree will sway. There is also the growth of the tree to consider. This is outward instead of simply upward, so while the tree house will rise over time it will also need to allow for the expansion of the tree.

Avoiding Accidents

In the excitement of planning and making a tree house, it is easy to forget that without care it can be a danger to both the occupants and the builders. Some risks are obvious, such as the risk of falling, while others are more unexpected. We have listed areas that can cause concern below. It is not an exhaustive list, so make sure that you check for hazards throughout the life of your tree house.

PLANNING AND LOCATION

Ensure that you are allowed to build where you intend to. Find out if there are any local regulations that prohibit building a tree house. Often smaller tree houses are not included in building regulations, but the tree may be protected. Talk to your neighbors to make sure that they are happy with your plans and that they have no grounds for objection.

Consider the strength and suitability of the tree; apart from the weight of the tree house, the tree must be able to withstand the added wind resistance that a structure will impose on it.

If you live in an area that has overhead power lines, never build in a tree within reach of them or underneath them. Make sure that the tree is far enough away so that anything the occupants do will not risk electric shock.

Consider design issues, such as providing sufficient headroom and having enough space to safely clear the ladder when entering and leaving. Avoid any swinging or loose wood that may catch the wind and cause injury.

POISONOUS PLANTS AND TREES

Some types of trees and plants that may be found in the vicinity of your tree house can be hazardous. Yew tree bark and needles are toxic on contact, and the berries can pose a serious danger if eaten. Laburnum seeds can tempt children to eat them with disastrous results. Other plants to look out for include box, deadly nightshade, leylandii, horse chestnut, and the common cherry laurel. If you are unsure about the tree that you will be using, seek advice.

ACTUAL SAFETY

It can be more dangerous to provide a solid-looking rail or guard that is actually too weak to prevent a fall than to leave the space open. Every guard that you build must be trustworthy. Keep in mind that people often behave far more cautiously if they feel insecure, so providing strong guards that appear insubstantial, such as netting, can take advantage of this added caution.

WHILE BUILDING

Keep the site orderly and clear. Make sure that you have space to work and that the items that you are working on are well supported. A solid, uncluttered work surface or bench at waist height will greatly speed up your work. Keep your wood and scraps separate from the making area and keep the tools that you are not using together in a central spot.

WORKING WITH MATERIALS

Be aware of any risks associated with the materials that you are using and take appropriate precautions when using them, such as wearing gloves, a mask, and protective goggles. Pay particular attention to hidden risks—for example, you should always wear a mask when cutting manufactured boards, such as plywood.

below Your working area should always be neat and uncluttered.

WORKING FROM THE PLATFORM

Make sure that all work carried out on the tree is done safely. Always remember the following safety guidelines:

• Ladders should extend beyond the height to be worked at; be based on firm ground at 75 degrees; rest firmly against a solid support; and, if possible, be securely tied. A ladder should never hold more than one person. Never attempt to overreach from the ladder.

• If the tree house is above head height, use rope and a pulley to hoist materials up to the platform. Before you transfer from working from the ladder to working on the platform, thoroughly check that the platform is secure.

• Use a tool belt to hold tools while you are not using them. If necessary, make a secure temporary location for tools and fasteners that you will need up the tree.

• Ensure that nothing can fall from the tree house level down onto people below.

• Take every available precaution to minimize the risk of falls. Consider renting special equipment and, if in doubt, seek advice or professional assistance.

• Ensure that the area beneath the tree-house site is always uncluttered and clear of dangerous rocks or stumps.

• Designate a single person to act as supervisor on the ground below the tree. This person will be responsible for controlling all ground operations and for carefully directing

left *Tree-house ladders should be installed only on firm, level ground. If necessary, spend some time preparing the area.*

SAFETY AND POWER TOOLS

Power tools should always be used with care. Follow the manufacturer's instructions and be sure to wear any advised safety equipment. Avoid using any power tool with its switch locked on and always keep the moving parts away from the body. Chain saws are particularly dangerous and should not be used unless you have received training and are wearing a complete safety outfit.

Make sure that any power you need is supplied via a circuit breaker at the source. Rain and damp grass can pose an unexpected threat when using power outside.

the movement of all people below the tree. They should also take full responsibility for ensuring clear communication with the people working above.

FOR THE OCCUPANTS

You must be absolutely sure that the tree house is structurally sound before use. Again, there are basic guidelines to follow:

- Make sure that there is a safe method of access to the tree. Ladders must be sturdy and secure when in position. If the tree itself is to be climbed, supplement any suspect sections of the climb with fabricated steps and handholds. If the vicinity could be muddy, provide a boot-cleaning area below the ascent point.

- Avoid the risk of falls at all costs. Ensure that all boards, rails, and platforms will not to move when weight is applied.

- Be sure that the area below the tree house is uncluttered, and clear of any rocks and stumps. Remove any stumps and snags from the trunk and branches below the tree house.

- Remove from the structure any sharp corners or pieces of wood that can cause splinters. If the removal causes any weakness in the structure, replace that part. Protruding screws or nails should be bent and sanded flat, or replaced.

- If your tree house has any hanging ropes, make sure that they are securely attached and that there is no potential for someone to get caught in them.

- Check for gaps in which someone might get their hands or head stuck—the gaps between any uprights on the rails are prone to this hazard. Enlarge the gaps or fill them.

- Be extra careful of any gaps between the tree house and the tree, especially where the two move independently. These gaps should be guarded.

WHAT TO LOOK FOR WHEN INSPECTING AN AGING TREE HOUSE

The lifespan of a tree house depends on a number of factors: the quality of the wood used in its construction; the care taken in applying preservation treatments; how water and ventilation are managed; its exposure to the weather and pests; and the nature of the fasteners used.

Never be complacent about a tree house's state of repair: if it was made cheaply, don't trust it to last for more than a season. Give it a thorough inspection regularly, and be prepared to dismantle it when it has reached the end of its useful life. Look on the dismantling as a great opportunity to build a more exciting and ambitious tree house that will enable you to increase your tree-house-building expertise.

- Make sure that the ends of any poles, sticks, or branches that could get in someone's eye are removed or made conspicuous. Make them a bright color or add a protective cap.

- Cover any timber or wood that has been previously treated with creosote so that direct skin contact is not possible. Creosote is often prohibited from use in playgrounds or places where regular skin contact is likely.

CARE AND MAINTENANCE

Check the tree house regularly, at least at the beginning and end of each season. Check for split wood, rotten wood, delaminated or peeling boards, corroding screws, bolts, and fasteners, fraying rope, and corroded cable. Replace anything that looks doubtful. Check the tree for signs of rot or ill health, and if it compromises the strength of your structure, either relocate the supports or dismantle the tree house.

Trees

Trees are an essential part of our environment. They have an importance to people everywhere, both in the huge variety of uses to which they are put and in the beliefs and myths

that we attach to them. For example, any Scottish person will tell you that a rowan tree must not be cut down because it protects the occupants of the land it is rooted in, and that its berries make a delicious condiment. To do justice to this body of knowledge would take up too much room here. Likewise, listing all the varieties of trees you might encounter would leave little room for the subject of the book. We have outlined the key issues that are specific to tree-house building. It is a good idea to find out as much as you can about any type of tree that you intend to build in by reading any of the many books available that deal with species, cultivation, and folklore.

left *Not all trees are as beautifully balanced as this one, but each deserves careful appraisal when considering where to place your tree house.*

HOW TREES WORK

From an engineer's point of view, each tree consists of various parts that all work together. The roots anchor the tree firmly to the ground, and will only be as firm as the surrounding soil. As a rule, the roots extend out from the tree as far as the leaf canopy stretches out above, and they supply the tree with nutrients from the outer edges of this area. Roots are fragile, especially when they are small, and you should always avoid damaging them.

THE TRUNK

The trunk of the tree has a center of hard, old heartwood surrounded by newer sapwood. This central core of solid wood has been built up over the years and provides the supporting strength of the tree. It has stopped growing. This is the wood that is used for the lumber you might buy.

Surrounding the sapwood, below the bark, is a microscopic wet layer called the cambium layer. This is where the tree's growth takes place, as new wood is slowly built up around the central core. The cambium layer is effectively a pipe that allows for the massive flow of liquid nutrients up the tree. It is also the living part of the tree's trunk. Any damage done to this layer will affect the tree. Bark covers the cambium layer, acting as a protective coating in a similar way to human skin. A tree's bark is a sacrificial dead layer that defends the tree, and if the bark is breached, the tree will do its best to replace it.

left *Always consider how a tree house will affect your view before beginning your project.*

THE BRANCHES

A mature tree's trunk grows in girth, becoming fatter but not higher. Extending the reach of the tree is the job of the branches and shoots. The main branches of the tree consist of exactly the same parts as the trunk, and can be thought of as minor trunks. They started life as small shoots growing lengthwise away from the tree and have gradually stopped getting longer as new shoots have, in turn, come from them. Because of this slow addition of wood, a tree's branches are rooted deeply into the early solid wood of the tree. The tree has had time to build up strength where it is needed by adding buttresses of extra wood at the points where the branches meet the trunk and the load is great. Sometimes a tree will put on new growth that is too heavy for these joints, causing the branch to drop under stress.

Farther up the tree, a huge number of small branches and shoots support the leaf canopy. The weight of these branches

TREES

21

and the massive added stress imposed by the wind demand great strength of the tree. To accommodate this weight and stress, the branches grow increasingly flexible as they get farther from the trunk, so that they can turn in the wind. The leaves are also formed to collapse temporarily in winds to reduce drag.

A tree is an extraordinary mechanism. It manages the weight of all that wood, the rigors of the weather, and the tons of fluid traveling around it. It burrows, irrigates, refines, and reproduces. Our best attempts to add another function to a tree will always be relatively primitive, but if we are careful and respectful, we can at least make sure not to interfere with its workings.

right *The cambium layer was breached when a branch was removed from this trunk. The tree has since grown a protective ring of bark to seal off the damage, leaving only the dead heartwood exposed.*

far right *A tree grows to accommodate the load it has to carry: kinks in this trunk were formed to balance branches long since removed.*

right *Buttresses slowly develop at the base of the tree in order to support the increasing strain on the trunk as the tree grows into full maturity.*

left *Building a tree house should have as little as possible impact on the tree and its immediate environment.*

Materials

WOOD

The type of wood you use to build your tree house depends on what is available to you. Most lumberyards sell perfectly adequate pine. Make sure that you choose straight, relatively knot-free lumber, and treat it with an exterior-grade preservative if it's not pressure-treated. For larger sizes, you can specify the quality of the wood for structural beams.

Softwood "boards" are sold by the actual length—or running or linear foot—while softwood dimensional lumber is sold by the board foot, a unit that is 12 inches long and wide and 1 inch thick, making up 144 cubic inches. Softwood boards come in sizes from 1 x 2 inches, referred to as 1 x 2s, up to 1 x 12 inches, or 1 x 12s. Dimensional lumber ranges from 2 x 2 inches up to 4 x 12 inches, or 2 x 2s to 4 x 12s. However, these measurements are nominal sizes—the size the wood was before planing—and the actual measurements are ¼ inch to ¾ inch smaller. Planed hardwood is ¼ inch thinner than the nominal size, and measurments are given in ¼-inch increments, from 4/4, which is 1-inch thick, to 8/4, which is 2 inches thick.

MANUFACTURED BOARDS

The most important consideration for the boards that you use their need to be weatherproof. If you want your tree house to las buy the best-quality marine plywood. Exterior-grade and weathe resistant plywood boards will not last as long. CDX plywood c moisture-resistant oriented strand board (or OSB) should be goo for a few years if you protect it well, especially at the edges. Board that take any weight, such as platform bases, must be at leas ¾-inch thick. Walls and roofs can be thinner.

JOINING WOOD TO WOOD

Nails are the most basic, but weakest method of joining woo to wood. To strengthen a nailed joint, drive the nail in at a angle. To make it even stronger, clinch it by using nails that ar long enough to protrude through the wood, then bend th protruding ends over. Flatten the sharp ends well into the woo

Screws make strong fasteners if used correctly. A screw should push easily through the topmost piece of wood an twist smoothly into the wood beneath until it pulls the two pieces tightly together. If the screw turns too easily or too tightly, it is not a good fastener. It should get tighter as the head presses harder against the wood. To make a good fastening, drill a hole in the uppermost wood so that you can push the screw through. In the wood beneath, drill a pilot hole that is smaller than the screw. Use clamps to hold wood together while adding screws.

JOINTS IN WOOD

These two joints are very useful for constructing a tree house:

DADO JOINT

This joint is used where two pieces of wood meet at right angles. The end of one piece of wood is housed in a groove made into a second piece. The end profile of the first piece is drawn on the face of the second piece. Wood is then removed to the desired depth, so that the two pieces slot together.

LAP JOINT

This joint is used where two pieces of wood cross each other. Two overlapping pieces of wood are altered to intersect by removing half of the thickness from each. The profile of each piece of wood is drawn onto both sides of the other piece where they cross. Half of the smaller piece of wood's thickness is then removed between these marks. The second piece is cut with a similar groove to hold the remaining wood on the first piece.

THE SECRET TO MAKING GOOD JOINTS

Accurately mark out both pieces of wood to be joined so you clearly understand what needs to be removed from each. Use lines to show where the wood intersects and shade areas where the wood is to be removed. First use a saw to cut any lines that cross the grain. Then use a chisel and mallet to split the wood along the grain between the saw cuts, removing small blocks of wood until you reach your line. Once the pieces are cut, do a dry run to test fit the components to make sure the joints fit snugly and the pieces are the correct size.

BASIC TERMINOLOGY

In this book, the following terms refer to the different sides of a piece of wood:

- **FACE:** longest, widest face.

- **SIDE:** longest, thinnest face.

- **EDGE:** angle where face and side meet.

- **ENDS:** small faces at either end.

- **CORNERS:** points where three faces meet.

For screwing instructions, we have used: "Screw part A to part B," meaning screw through part A into part B. The heads of the screws will be on the surface of part A.

JOINING WOOD TO THE TREE

Although trees are made of wood, you must choose a fastening technique that protects the living tree. If you are certain that the part you are attaching to is dead and it is solid enough to bear weight, you can use screws and joints to make the fastening. It is more likely that the part of the tree you use is live, in which case the objective is to minimize damage to the tree. One or two long bolts will be enough to attach a solid piece of wood, which you can then attach others to. This piece of wood should be firmly secured to the tree with bolts so that it cannot rub against the bark and cause damage.

MATERIALS

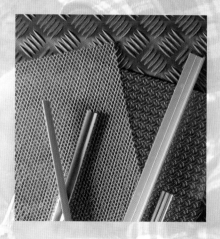
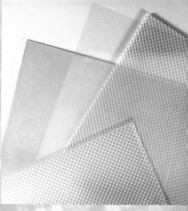

PLASTICS AND OTHER MATERIALS

above Secure metal treads to floors and to rungs for extra traction, or use metal mesh to cover spy holes cut through the floor. Remember to file down any sharp edges.

Few plastic materials are rigid enough for supporting elements, but many make excellent covers and canopies. Clear, rigid plastics, such as acrylic and polycarbonate sheets, make ideal replacements for window panes, and plastic film can be stretched to form elegant, tentlike roofs. If you want to use the tree house in the winter, you can use expanded foam products, such as polyurethane, for insulation.

METALS

If you have experience in metalworking, it may be worth making special brackets for improving a wooden structure. Replacing the structure itself with metal beams can be too heavy for serious consideration. Sheet materials, such as corrugated iron and tinplate, can make good wall panels and roofs. They can be secured with screws in the same way as wood.

CABLE ROPE AND CHAIN

Rope comes in two main forms useful for constructing a tree house. The plastic and jute ropes that most people are familiar with are good for suspending parts of the tree house and for climbing. These traditional ropes come in many types, textures and colors. Wire rope is extremely strong in tension and can be used to support large loads; in theory, an ⅛-inch wire rope can support half a ton. It is easily secured using standard fasteners and is long-lasting if you use a stainless steel variety. It is essential to ensure that any rope you use is strong enough to support its load and that all knots or fasteners are adequate.

Chain can be used to suspend elements of the treehouse and to form barriers. It has the advantage that you can connect multiple lengths from a single link point and connections can be made easily using shackles and "rapide" links. As with ropes, you must ensure that any chain and fixings are strong enough. Never use any chain without closed or welded links.

JOINING CABLE AND ROPE

Wire rope must always be joined by mechanical fasteners. The required length of rope is made into a sling with a loop or thimble at each end. These thimbles are used to connect the sling to the attachments points using shackles, tensioners and, if needed, swivels. The sling is made by passing a loop o wire around a thimble and then securing the free end back to the main run using at least three wire rope clamps or ferrules.

Chain is best connected using a "quick" link. This fastener has a screwable section that allows for the link to be looped into the main chain. Shackles work in a similar way, but are preferred for joining several chains to a single point.

Fiber rope can only be formed into slings with thimbles by splicing. Only attempt this operation if you are skilled. Fiber ropes can be used for less critical loads (ladders, swings, lashings) by using knots. You will need a separate reference book on knots if you want to make them central to your construction.

KNOTS

Using rope to secure parts of the structure can add to the visual appeal of your tree house. Knots are not integral to the projects in this book, but you may decide to include them in some of your designs. If your tree house takes the form of a ship, using rigging to secure masts and spars will help your craft look authentic. Lengths of rope can also adorn and support a jungle lodge or rain-forest retreat effectively. You can even learn to make your own rope ladders using knots.

If knots are used to support any parts of the structure, you must ensure that they are safe and secure. It is worth studying a separate reference book, because there are so many variations. One example, a round turn and two half hitches, is shown here. You can use this knot to temporarily fasten a rope to a post:

1. Wrap the rope around the post for two complete turns.

2. Pass the working end of the rope over and around the standing part, then feed it between the post and the standing part.

3. Bring the working end away from the post and make another wrap around the standing part, feeding the working end between the previous wrap and the standing part.

4. Pull on the working end and cinch the knot up to the post to tighten.

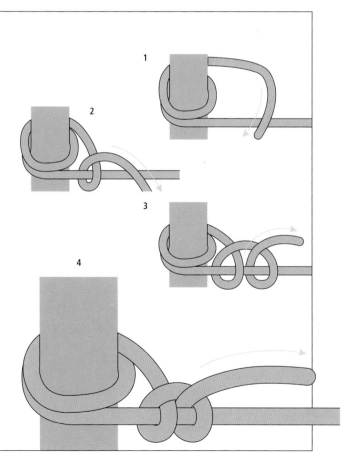

FASTENERS: SCREWS AND BOLTS

Screws come in various sizes and qualities. Be sure that you buy the best available. We have used no. 8 Phillips screws for most of the work in this book, but if your tree house is larger, use thicker screws. As a rule, any screw used should be long enough to pass through the first piece of wood with at least two-thirds of the screw projecting into the piece it is being secured to.

right It is essential to choose the correct size of screw for each task.

BOLTS

There are two types of bolts: those with self-tapping threads and those with parallel threads that require nuts. Use self-tapping bolts for securing into trees. Use bolts with nuts for attaching to any lumber that you can drill clear through. Always use washers under the heads and nuts of any bolts. If you need to allow for movement, use a spring or rubber washer.

CABLE FASTENERS

Fasteners for cables usually consist of eyebolts. These can be purchased with nuts, or with screw threads as screw eyes. They do not need washers under the eye. To tighten them, use a length of steel bar, such as a screwdriver, passed through the eye as a lever. Never attach cable by looping it over a branch or any other wood. It will fray or cut through the tree's protective bark over time.

SECURING TO THE GROUND

A ground anchor is the best fastener for securing to the ground. There are many types of anchors. One effective type resembles a large corkscrew screwed into the ground.

GLOSSARY

ANNULAR RING NAIL
A nail with sharp rings along its length to prevent it from being pulled out easily.

CARRIAGE BOLT
A long bolt that has a parallel thread and is used with a nut. It does not usually have a hexagonal end; instead, a carriage bolt has a domed end, and because of this it cannot be tightened from the bolt end.

CLINCHING
The technique of making a nail tightly secured by using a nail long enough to protrude through the material to be joined, and then bending the sharp end over so that it lies flat.

EYEBOLT
A bolt with a parallel thread that has a ring. or "eye," for a head. It is used with a nut and washer and usually forms a locating point for hooks or chains.

FLUSH
A term to express the fact that two or more objects are aligned so that neither protrudes more than the other.

GFI
A ground fault interrupter, also known as a GFI, measures inequalities in the supply and return of electrical power and halts the supply in a fraction of a second if current is leaking. The speed of the cut off is such that electric shocks can be avoided. When using power tool equipment in a workshop or outdoors, or in areas around water, using a GFI is strongly recommended.

KERFING
A technique for bending solid wood that involves cutting a repeated series of parallel lines, which weaken the wood enough to facilitate bending.

LAP JOINT
A type of wood joint where half of each piece of wood to be joined is removed to accept the remaining half of the other.

LEVEL
A term that describes a surface that has no slope. It is also used to describe two or more horizontal points or marks where no surface joins them together.

LOCKNUT
A type of nut used to lock a bolt fastener so that it cannot work loose. Locknuts can be in the form of a second nut tightened onto the first, or a special nut with a nylon insert.

PILOT HOLE
Any small hole that is used as a guide hole for a subsequent insertion. Pilot holes are drilled to allow for the easy drilling of much larger holes and for the easy insertion of screws.

QUICK LINK
A type of removable chain link that has a section that can be unscrewed for removal and tightened for safety.

SCREW EYE
A screw eye is similar to an eyebolt in having a closed ring as its head. The difference is that it has a self-tapping screw thread instead of a parallel thread; therefore, it can be screwed into wood without the need for a nut.

SCRIM
A loose-woven cloth made from rough fibers that is used to support plaster or any moldable material.

SELF-TAPPING THREAD
A sharp, helical thread, commonly found on wood screws, that cuts a groove for itself as it is turned, thus pulling itself deeper into the material until tight against the head.

SHACKLES
U-shaped fasteners with removable closing attachments. Shackles are used as removable links in rigging and climbing.

SPACER
A term for a piece of material that is used solely to fill a gap.

SPLICING
The joining of two pieces of rope by unwinding their strands and then winding them together again to make an invisible and inherent joint.

SPRING WASHER
A washer in the form of a helix or shallow spring, used to provide a slight amount of movement without slackness.

SQUARE
A term that has come to mean anything that is aligned accurately at 90 degrees (right angles), based on the fact that squares have even sides and angles. It can also refer to a structure that is not bent or twisted in any way.

TENSIONER
A tensioner is a device that gets longer or shorter as it is turned. In this way, it can be used to loosen or tighten a line or cable.

THIMBLE
A teardrop-shaped loop of metal that is used to strengthen and protect loops in wire and fiber rope.

WIRE ROPE CLAMP
A device for clamping two sections of wire rope together firmly. Sometimes called a wire rope clip or U-bolt grip, it is constructed from a bent U-shaped piece of steel with a thread at either end and a forged saddle that threads over the ends of the steel U. Nuts are used to tighten the saddle, which acts as the clamp.

Tools

TOOLS FOR MARKING OUT

There are a variety of tools that can be used for marking out, each with its own advantages and disadvantages:

KNIFE
A sharp knife is the most accurate marker, but its mark will only be visible on well-surfaced wood.

PENCIL AND MARKER PEN
A sharp pencil is accurate and visible on most wood. Reserve a marker pen more for guessing than for accurate marking; however, it is essential for marking out the tree and its bark.

TAPE MEASURE
Because tape measures are prone to twisting and being misread. The most accurate way to transfer a measurement is to hold the object where you want it and mark it off. Or mark the important length on a spare piece of wood and use it as a customized ruler. For some applications, however, only a tape measure will do.

DUCT TAPE OR CARPET TAPE
Duct or carpet tape is especially useful for marking out trees You can adhere it over rough bark in the place you want to mark and then add a more precise indication with a marker pen. The tape will be visible from a distance when a mark directly on the tree will not.

TRY SQUARE
A try square, sometimes just called a square, is used for marking right angles across components and for checking that posts and rails are "square" to each other. The blade rests flat on the component that is to be marked.

LEVEL
A level contains a small bubble that you align between two marks to check that a surface is level. It prevents sloping horizontals and ensures uprights are vertical. It can be rested across separate items to check that they are aligned.

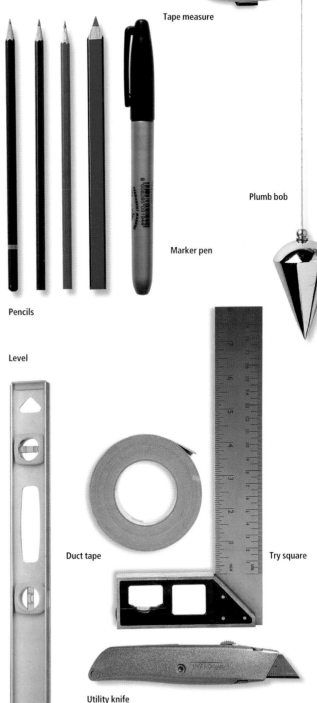

WATER LEVEL

A water level or pipe level is used in the same way as a level but over longer distances. Instead of using a bubble, the water surfaces are aligned at both ends of a tube full of water. This tool can be made from a length of clear tube. *(See also page 115.)*

PLUMB BOB

A plumb bob is a length of string with a weight on the end. When it is hung from a point it gives a vertical line and will indicate the spot directly below the hung point. This tool can be a home-made contraption but the weight must be centered on the string. Chalk lines often have plumb bobs attached.

Tape measure

Plumb bob

Marker pen

Pencils

SIMPLE RULES FOR ACCURATE MARKING

Accurate marking is the secret of most successful projects. It is easy if you follow a few simple rules:

- Always use a sharp pencil or even a knife, so that there will be no doubt as to which side of the line is important.

- Always measure along one edge of the wood. The edge is a convenient line that will make an exact point when you draw your measurement line across it.

- When marking from a tape measure, make it clear which end of the mark was closest to the measure by giving it a tail or arrow. This way you will know which is the accurate end of the mark.

- Once you have transferred the measurement, use a square to mark a straight line across the whole face of the wood that you are marking. Then work to this new neat line.

- When you mark a length of wood or beam, always use a square to draw a line from the edge right across one face, then make another line from that same edge across the other face. You should have a line that wraps halfway around the whole piece. To test your accuracy, try joining them up at the opposite corner.

- Whenever you are making a mark to fit another item, it is more accurate to hold the item up to the wood you are marking than to use a tape measure.

Level

Duct tape

Try square

Utility knife

33

TOOLS FOR CUTTING AND SECURING

The correct tools are essential to accurate cutting, which in turn is key to creating an attractive construction:

HANDSAWS

A crosscut saw or panel saw is the most appropriate tool for cutting boards and lumber. A tenon saw (with a thick spine along the top of a short, rectangular blade) can be used for cutting joints but is not essential. Use a hacksaw to cut metal.

HOLE SAWS

Hole saws usually come with a number of different-size circular blades that fit into a power drill. They are used to make round holes and rounded corners for openings in board.

WOOD CHISELS

Chisels are used for finishing off joints by cutting away wood along the grain, often between two saw cuts. For these projects, a wide-bevel chisel is needed, used with a mallet. Always keep the chisel sharp.

TIPS FOR SAWING

When using a handsaw, always point the index finger of the hand holding the saw along the blade. This will make the saw more controllable and the cut will be more accurate.

- It is always more accurate to cut to a line. Try to cut exactly next to it, so that you can still see it when you are done.

- When starting a saw cut, begin with the blade resting on a corner and slowly pull the saw toward you a few times. Saws are designed to cut on the push stroke, so the less aggressive action of pulling the saw will start the cut without it jamming.

- For accurate joints, always start to cut from the far corner first, then slowly level the saw until it runs along the line drawn across the top surface. The straight blade will ensure a straight cut along the top, so you can concentrate on keeping the vertical cut straight.

- The weight of a saw is enough to do all the cutting, so there is no need to push down. Instead, try to set up a gentle rhythm that uses the whole length of the blade.

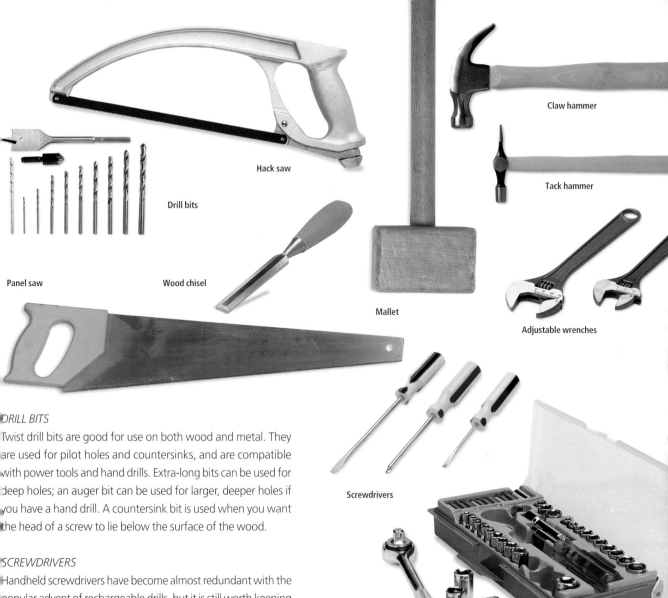

Hack saw

Drill bits

Claw hammer

Tack hammer

Panel saw

Wood chisel

Mallet

Adjustable wrenches

Screwdrivers

Socket wrench set

DRILL BITS

Twist drill bits are good for use on both wood and metal. They are used for pilot holes and countersinks, and are compatible with power tools and hand drills. Extra-long bits can be used for deep holes; an auger bit can be used for larger, deeper holes if you have a hand drill. A countersink bit is used when you want the head of a screw to lie below the surface of the wood.

SCREWDRIVERS

Handheld screwdrivers have become almost redundant with the popular advent of rechargeable drills, but it is still worth keeping a screwdriver in your toolbox for hard-to-reach corners. Phillips screwdrivers are most often used.

WRENCHES

Wrenches are needed for securing bolts and tightening cable cleats. Ensure that you have the sizes you need for the bolts you have. Box-end wrenches, open-end wrenches, or socket wrenches will do. A rachet wrench is good for cable cleats.

HAMMER

A claw hammer is an essential tool that can be used for a wide variety of jobs. It is an ideal weight for most nails and can be used to remove nails and damaged screws. It also makes a good, all-purpose, prying tool. Tack hammers are good for small nails.

TOOLS

POWER TOOLS AND ADDITIONAL TOOLS

While there is something special about using hand tools to work wood, power tools can save a lot of time and effort:

RECHARGEABLE DRILL OR SCREWDRIVER
A rechargeable drill can be used as both a drill and a screwdriver, and lets you work in places where it is not possible to get power. The higher the voltage of the battery, the better the drill will perform. Have spare batteries at hand.

SABER SAW
A saber saw, or jigsaw, lets you make curved cuts in board to match a tree's profile as well as managing a variety of decorative work that cannot be done easily any other way.

NAIL GUN
A nail gun can be a great time saver for securing board and adding surface elements, but it should not be used to substitute nails for the screws specified in these instructions.

POWER MITER SAW
A power miter saw, or any other bench saw, will save time when accurately cutting the wood for your tree house. However, it is not an essential item as it is often quicker to cut wood by hand, on site, than to move it to the machine.

Rechargeable drill

Power extension cord

Spade

Pruning shears

Lopping shears

Saber saw

Brushes and rollers

BOW SAW, PRUNING SAW, AND SHEARS

Use a bow saw for clearing away tree growth; it will not bind in the wet wood of the tree like a carpenter's saw. Clear away small branches with a pruning saw, pruning shears, or lopping shears.

AX

A small ax is useful for clearing away dead wood on a stump or for leveling an area of dead branches.

SPADE

A spade is useful for leveling ground or for seating footing slabs.

POWER EXTENSION CORD

Make sure your extension cord a ground fault interrupter (GFI) to avoid electric shock. Always unroll it fully, and do not plug cords together to make them longer.

ROLLERS AND BRUSHES

Having a cheap assortment of these for decorating will help keep colors separate and avoid the need for frequent cleaning.

Taking it Further

Once you understand the function of each part of a tree house structure, customization is possible by making changes to one or more of these parts.

BASIC FUNCTIONS

You can adapt and expand the various parts of a tree house, as long as you ensure that their basic functions are not compromised. The basic functions of the various parts are:

FASTENERS
To support weight and allow for movement while protecting the tree.

PLATFORM
To provide a totally stable base for the occupants and for other elements, such as the walls, roof, and furniture.

WALLS
To prevent falls, and to provide shelter and a sense of enclosure.

ROOF
To protect from sunlight and other weather.

It is worth considering what you can change or improve as you discover more elegant ways to integrate your tree house into its specific location. As well as pointing out solutions to problems before they occur, imagining the parts of the tree house before you build it lets you explore creative alternatives without the expense of making changes midway through building.

The best way to imagine the structure is to draw sketches, make cardboard modelsm or even use wood to make small-scale versions—use any means that you want.

IMAGINATION

The process of planning can be a lot of fun, especially if you le your imagination run away with you. It may sound impractica but one of the best techniques for thinking creatively abou structures is to imagine something to an impossible extrem and then adjust the change bit by bit until it is possible (all th while staying alert for interesting ideas).

Take the fasteners, for instance. The function of fastener is to provide secure attachments to the tree. They must b as strong as possible without harming the tree. Imagin something that is as strong as the tree itself and completel compatible with it—its own branches perhaps? An extrem solution would be to actually train the tree to grow into a tree house shape, grafting or weaving live branches as needed. I would make an amazing, if long-term, project.

To adjust the idea, there might well be branches that coul be redirected to form a roof or used directly as supportin beams. Perhaps you could add false, branch-shape element to give the tree house a cartoonlike appearance. At the ver least, looking at the branches of the tree will give you insight into the best shapes and position for fasteners. Topiary migh also be used to complement the look of the structure. Bushe could be planted among the supports to gradually form integra parts of the tree house.

Although these kind of imaginative games might seem at first, like a wasteful diversion, they can actually show yo practical ways to save time and materials.

INSPIRATION

If you don't come up with your own ideas, seek inspiration Open a book or a magazine at random and try to incorporat whatever you find into your line of thinking. The more unlikel the subject, the better the chance that you will surprise yourself. Let the words or images you find suggest things to you. If you reveal a person, imagine you are making the tree house for him or her. If you reveal a fictional situation, use the atmosphere or events as your inspiration. The most obscure idea can take you away from habitual and familiar ways of thinking, forcing you to see things from a new perspective. Often, this approach will highlight the things that are really important to you.

Once you have decided on an idea, mark it as option A, then start again to come up with B and again for C. The first idea is often the most experimental and each successive one can be an improvement. A final trick is to imagine the opposite of the subject or theme you like. Do this in terms of style, dimensions, materials, and approach; in fact, consider any kind of opposite you can invent.

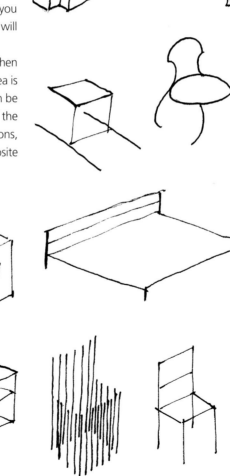

right and above Even a simple chair shape can offer limitless possibilities for imaginative design when slight alterations are made or aspects are exaggerated.

TREE HOUSES
FOR TREES WITH STRAIGHT TRUNKS AND NO FORKS

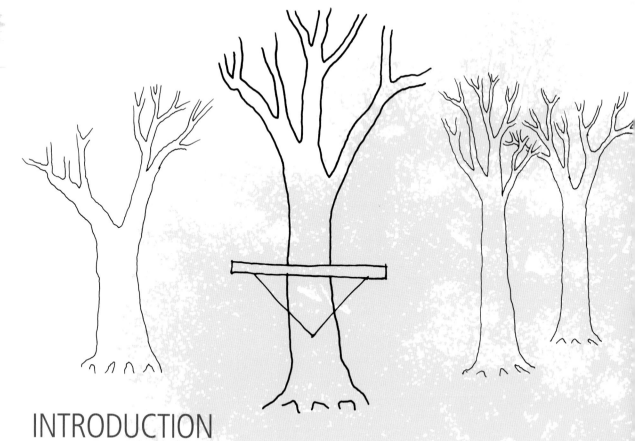

INTRODUCTION

The tree houses in this section are for trees with a single, straight trunk without large forks or branches. You can convert them to fit any other type of tree with a bit of ingenuity and a good look at the other sections in this book.

Building a tree house on a single, straight tree has one advantage and one minor difficulty. The advantage is that there is not much extra tree to get in the way of your creation, so you can let your imagination run wild without *having to curb your designs because of an intrusive branch. The difficulty is that you must attach your tree house extremely carefully. You only have one place to attach the platform, so it must be done well. Fortunately, on a single, straight trunk, it is easier to ensure that the fasteners are sound, and the lack of clutter will give you a lot of space to work in. This section introduces four different structures: two without legs and two with grounded supports.*

POSSIBLE PLATFORMS

The success of any tree house depends on the platform it rests on. The actual appearance of the tree house is normally cosmetic dressing added later. In this section, we begin by giving detailed information on how to create a basic platform on a single, straight tree. Here, you will find basic skills that can be used when building any kind of tree-house structure.

Straight-trunk tree houses only have a single pole to brace themselves on, so keeping them stable can be something of a structural challenge. Luckily, there are a variety of ways to improve stability, including using the ground for support and hanging the platform from branches.

STANDING AND HANGING

Adding legs that rest on firm ground can be an excellent way of increasing the size of tree house accommodated by a single tree. At its most extreme, this approach can lead to tree houses that don't touch the tree they are associated with. Similar to houses on stilts built around a tree, these tree houses have structural demands that can be solved using conventional building techniques. When adding a "leg" to a tree house, foundations become an issue. The footing should make a solid base, and can be a slab of rock set on firm ground. If the tree house is not too large, it can be staked into the ground.

Hanging a tree house is not a common approach. At its simplest, it makes use of a convenient overhanging branch to take some of the weight from the far edges of the platform. At its most extreme, it uses high-tech materials to suspend a whole structure like a suspension bridge. When suspending, materials and fasteners must be approached differently. The weight that they bear pulls instead of pushes. In these situations, steel cable, chain, or polypropylene rope are far more suitable than wood. Fasteners and joints must be very secure to resist pulling free.

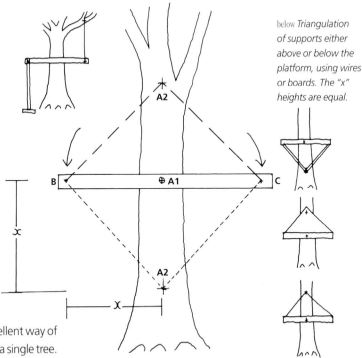

below *Triangulation of supports either above or below the platform, using wires or boards. The "x" heights are equal.*

THE SINGLE, STRAIGHT-TREE PLATFORM

A single, straight tree presents a particular challenge for fastening a platform. The tree is, in effect, a vertical pole. Any horizontal attachments will want to rotate around its fastening point, a bit like a balance. Even two or three bolts in the trunk at the same level from the ground will only act as a single fastening point.

The trick for a single, straight tree is to make sure that the platform is attached at two distant fastening points. The farther apart they are, the more stable the platform will be.

Because there is no nearby branch or trunk to brace to, the only option is to have one fastening point at platform level (A1) and a second (A2) below or above it. This second fastening point might be at ground level, high above the first—perhaps at a branch—or both.

The platform must be braced to these two fastening points using a diagonal support (connected to B and C). The trunk of the tree, the platform, and the diagonal support should form a large triangle. This triangle should be at least half as high as it is wide.

The Basic Platform

This platform was designed for a child's tree house. It is not very high off the ground (approximately 6½ feet), but even at this height there is a sense of being above everyone else, and the height can be adjusted to suit your needs. Every tree is different, so you will inevitably need to make some slight changes to these designs to suit the particular character of your tree.

MATERIALS NEEDED FOR
THE BASIC PLATFORM

Additional materials required for each project are listed on the relevant pages. For the basic platform, you will require:

2 main support beams: 2 x 4 inches x 8 feet
2 triangular supports: ¾-inch board
2 end beams: 2 x 4 x 48 inches
2 side beams: 2 x 2 inches x 8 feet
6 crossbeams: 2 x 2 x 48 inches
4 small support triangles: ¾-inch board
4 short wood strips to attach small triangles: 1 x 2 inches
Platform board: ¾ inch x 4 feet x 8 feet

FOR THE LADDER
(The length, number of rungs, and number of optional spacers
    will depend on the height of the tree)
2 posts: 2 x 2 inches x 10 feet or longer
10 or more rungs: 1 x 2 x 18 inches
20 or more spacers (optional): 1 x 2 x 10 inches
2 stakes: 2 x 2 inches

FASTENERS
4 bolts: ⅜-inch diameter, 6–8 inches long, with washers
Screws: 2–2¾ inches, assorted

(CUTTING PLAN: PAGE 147)

CHOOSING A TREE

First, choose your tree and the best position for your platform. The ideal tree has a straight trunk that is as vertical as possible. It is possible to accommodate a leaning tree with this design, but the straighter and more upright the tree the better. The platform will require a tall stretch of trunk about 45 inches long that has no branches or large bulges in it.

If your tree is smooth and consistently parallel from the ground to the branch base, then you can pick any height you want. If not, look for the longest clear stretch of smooth, parallel trunk on the tree and use this to set your height. Keep in mind that if the clear stretch you choose is only 45 inches long, the platform will be best set at the top of this clear stretch.

MARKING THE HEIGHT AND SETTING FASTENING POINTS

Mark the point on the tree where the platform level will be (there must be at least 45 inches clear below this point). Use duct tape to make the marking clear and repositionable. Wrap a piece of tape completely around the tree, trying to keep it as level and even as possible. The top of this band will mark the height of the platform.

Establish where the first bolts will be located. Walk around the tree to locate the point where the chosen section of trunk looks most vertical and mark both points where a level hole drilled from right to left would pierce the tape. Get these marks as level as possible; we will call them the "bolt marks" and they will be roughly where the first bolts should go. For later reference, stick a vertical line of tape straight down from each bolt mark using a level (or plumb bob).

THE MAIN SUPPORTS

Before attaching anything to the tree construct the main supports. There are two of these, each consisting of a triangle of board with a beam attached to its longest side.

Take two 8 foot-long lengths of 2 x 4s and, at the midpoint along the length of each beam, mark the center across the 2-inch and 4-inch faces.

Attach each of these beams to a triangle support. Center the beams on the long edge of the triangle. To do this, find the midpoint of the long edge of the triangle and mark it. Then lay the beam on its 4-inch face and place the triangle on top, so the midpoint marks align and the edge of the beam is flush with the edge of the triangle. Attach each triangle to its beam using eight equally spaced screws. Do not put a screw on the midpoint line, or it will get in the way later on.

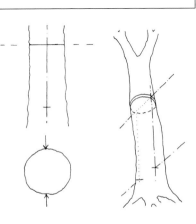

left *Marking the platform height and bolt locations using tape.*

right *Bolt marks must be level on opposite sides of the trunk, allowing for fastening through the thickest part of the tree.*

> ## UNEVEN TREES
>
> Trees come in all kinds of shapes and sizes. It is unlikely that you have the ideal trunk to start with. If your tree has an uneven trunk at the fastening points, you have the option to fill in any dips or cut off any bumps, or do a combination of both. You should only cut off any bumps or projecting branch stumps if you are sure that they are dead (they will be gray and without live bark). Dips can be filled in using pieces of wood (often several thin strips will be better than one thick piece). You will probably have enough odd bits of wood to choose from once you have begun cutting wood in preparation.

THE BASIC PLATFORM

ATTACHING THE TRIANGLE SUPPORTS

The triangular main supports that you have just made must be attached to the tree using bolts. These should be between 6 inches and 8 inches in length so that they can pass deep into the tree trunk. If the tree is thick, use the longer bolts.

Drill a hole for the bolt right through the support triangle and beam at the midpoint line. The hole should be wide enough to let the bolt slide in fairly easily without binding; use a drill the same thickness as the bolt.

Get someone to hold the first triangular support up against the tree where you want it to be, so that the hole you have just drilled lines up with one of the bolt marks on the tree. Now you will discover if any parts of the tree are in the way. If so, either trim the tree or make small alterations to the support by filling it out with some extra wood.

Once the hole in the support aligns neatly with the bolt marks you made on the tree previously, mark the exact location by hammering the bolt lightly into the bark. Remove the bolt and take the support away. You should now have a dent in the tree; drill the pilot hole there to the same depth as your bolt. Reposition the support beam, then insert the first bolt with a washer under its head and tighten it with a wrench until the washer is gripped against the wood.

Because the support is only held with one bolt at this stage, it should be easy to swivel the support until it is level. Once it is, do up the bolt tightly, checking all the time that it is level.

With your pilot drill, make a second hole at the bottom corner of the triangle toward the center of the tree. Ensure this hole is as deep as your bolt. Swivel the triangle and use the drill to widen the hole in the support (but not the tree) so that the bolt slips through it. Insert the second bolt and tighten fully. If the bottom of the triangle is too far away from the tree, fill the gap with a spare piece of drilled wood.

Attach the second support in the same way but first get your friend to hold it up while you check it is level across from the support you have just attached. Keep in mind that the supports will have a square floor resting on them, so it is important to get

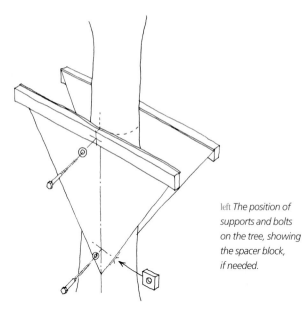

left *The position of supports and bolts on the tree, showing the spacer block, if needed.*

the ends of the beams parallel and as aligned as possible. You should now have two supports whose top surfaces are level in all directions. If not, you can always reattach one of the supports.

If either of the supports is outrageously crooked in relation to the tree, add some filling material to the bolt fastenings beneath the triangles. Use spare pieces of wood drilled with a bolt-size hole.

STRENGTHENING THE PLATFORM

Take the two 48 inch-long, 2 x 4 beams. Cut a notch at the top of each end to accommodate the 2 x 2 side beams that you will be attaching soon. Make sure that the notches are both on the same side of the beams.

Before you can attach these end beams, you need to cut similar lap joints in the ends of the supporting beams that you have already attached to the tree. Make the joints so the notches are uppermost. Once all four joints are cut on the support beams, rest one of the loose end beams in the new joints, making sure its notches are uppermost. Get the end beams to overhang the same amount on both sides (the amount of overhang depends on your tree's width). Mark where the end beams meet the support beams, then transfer these marks to the other loose beam and put it in place, too. The end beams should overhang the same amount as each other. Secure the beams in place by putting two screws through the joints in the support beams into the end beams.

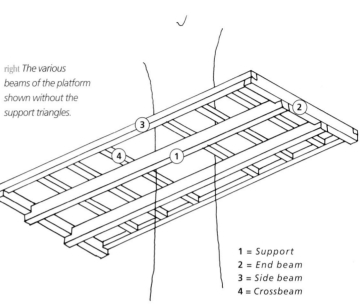

right *The various beams of the platform shown without the support triangles.*

1 = *Support*
2 = *End beam*
3 = *Side beam*
4 = *Crossbeam*

1. *Ensuring that the support is upright (this support needed spacing blocks).*

2 *Tightening the support bolt while checking for level.*

3. *Positioning the second support, using temporary wood strips to aid positioning.*

4. *Marking the lower bolt hole with the fill-in spacer.*

5. *Cutting notches on the top of the support beams to take the end beams.*

6. *Making sure the notches are level.*

THE BASIC PLATFORM

47

FITTING THE END BEAMS

To make the end beams fit perfectly, use them to measure from. Begin by resting one of the notched end beams where it will go, across both of the support beams, so that it is flush with both ends. Mark the width across the top of both support beams (this will give the exact thickness that the notch needs to be). Then use a square to continue these lines down each side face. Mark the height of the wooden lugs at the ends of each end beam from the top surface. This will give you the exact depth of the notches.

ATTACHING THE SIDE BEAMS AND CROSSBEAMS

Take two side beams (8-foot lengths of 2 x 2s) and sit them in the notches so they rest across the two end beams that were just attached. If they don't fit, you should be able to pull the end beams slightly closer or farther apart. Secure them in place at each joint using two screws down through the new side beams.

Cut six pieces of 2 x 2s long enough to rest across the side beams. Take two of these beams and rest them across the side beams on either side of the tree trunk. Make sure that they are 1 inch or so away from the tree trunk and parallel with the end beams. Mark exactly where they go and give each one an identifying letter: A, B, etc. Then mark how long they need to be to fit between the side beams, and cut them a tiny bit longer. Push them into position between the side beams.

Take another two crossbeams, space each evenly toward the end beam, and fit them in the same way. Do the same with the third pair of crossbeams on the other side of the trunk. Draw a line on the vertical side of the side beams indicating the center of each new crossbeam. Use screws to attach the crossbeams through the side beams at these new lines; they will also be needed later.

ATTACHING LATERAL SUPPORTS

Number each end of the crossbeams nearest to the tree trunk from one to four, then take the four smaller triangles and number them from one to four, too. Get the platform structure as level as possible. Hold up each of the triangle so that it rests against the large support triangle and presses against the edge of its corresponding crossbeam. You will need to cut corners into each triangle to allow for the 2 x 4 support beams. It is important that the triangles do not emerge above the platform level.

The triangles need to be a good fit—they should rest firmly against the large supporting triangles and take some of the weight from the platform. When you are sure that they are fitting well, attach them to the crossbeam using at least four screws evenly distributed along its length. Push the platform upward slightly to take up any sag when you attach them. Finally, use short wood strips to attach the smaller triangles firmly to the large supporting triangles (see panel).

1. *Attaching the end beams with screws through the supports.*

2. *The end beams and side beams in position.*

3. *The crossbeams in position.*

4. *The lateral supports in position (these curved supports are for the Pirate Ship).*

ATTACHING WITH STRIPS

To attach a small support triangle, ensure that it is vertically straight and draw a line on the large supporting triangle, using the smaller triangle as a rule. Attach a short wood strip to the large supporting triangle, using evenly spaced screws (remember to drill holes in the strip first). Attach the smaller triangle to the strip using evenly spaced screws through the side of the strip.

A PILOT HOLE

A pilot hole is a small hole that guides a bolt as it screws into a tree. It should be no thicker than half the thickness of the bolt or screw; the screw thread must bite into the wood of the tree.

below *Marking out the tree hole in the platform board. The distance of the gap 'N' can be used to find the thickness of the tree and the amount to be removed so that the board will slide around the trunk to fit.*

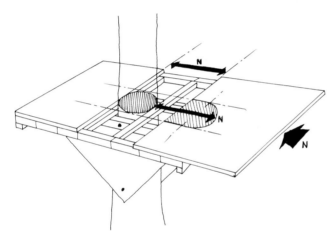

ATTACHING THE PLATFORM

Select one of the crossbeams closest to the tree trunk and locate the crossbeam center marks that you made earlier. Measure the distance from those marks to the outside edge of the nearest end beam. Transfer the measurements to a standard 4 x 8-foot board, making sure that the left-hand measurement is on the left and vice versa. Draw a straight line across the two measurements and saw the board along that line.

Take the shortest piece of board and place it on the structure. Its sawn edge should be nearest the tree and should run along the center of the crossbeam you first measured from.

Take the longer piece of board and put that in position as close as you can to the tree trunk, ensuring that the board edges line up along the side beams. Using a straight plank laid across the gap between the boards as a ruler, draw a pair of lines on the large board to show the thickness of the tree trunk.

Measure the gap between both parts of the board and mark it along both lines that you have just drawn. Join up both marks and you will have drawn the rectangle that needs to be removed so that the board will fit around the tree. Alternatively, draw freehand curve.

Cut the rectangle or semicircle away and slide the board around the tree until it reaches the other piece of board. If it doesn't fit, find the point that is stopping it, mark it on the board, and saw off more wood. Once the deck fits, secure it to all the supporting beams using evenly spaced screws.

FINISHING OFF

To finish the basic deck, make sure that you trim off any pieces of wood that protrude from the main platform. If they are left on, they will make adding additional elements more difficult later on. Now carefully check the platform for strength and stability. If it feels insecure, find any loose or poorly supported sections and add additional strengtheners or fasteners. Construction of the ladder is described in the following project.

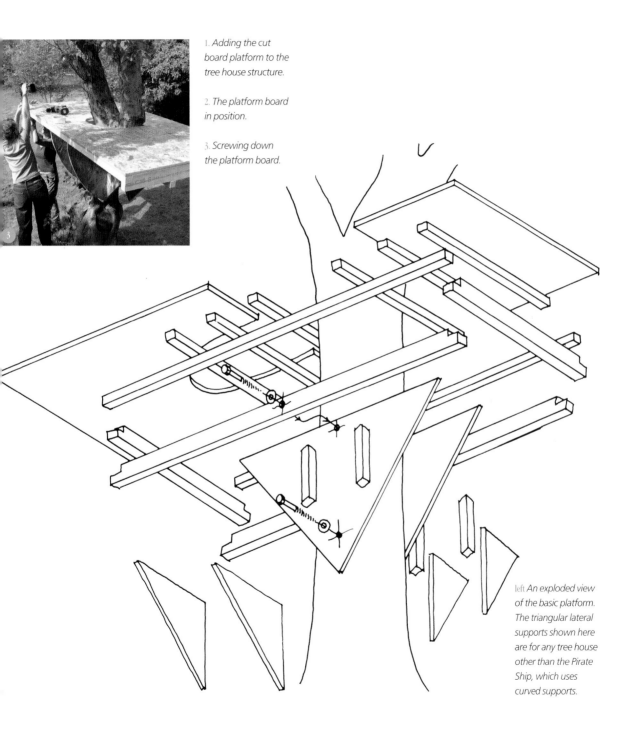

1. *Adding the cut board platform to the tree house structure.*

2. *The platform board in position.*

3. *Screwing down the platform board.*

left *An exploded view of the basic platform. The triangular lateral supports shown here are for any tree house other than the Pirate Ship, which uses curved supports.*

51

DESERT ISLAND LODGE

The Desert Island Lodge, based on the Basic Platform, is a simple tree house to build and can be easily converted to any theme, simply by adding decoration or elaborating on the materials used. Think of it as a stage set and be prepared to try out a variety of objects as decoration, such as driftwood, nets, and shells, or bind on exotic leaves. One of the joys of a

tree house is that it can be a secret retreat. As well as being used for imaginative play with others, it can also be a space for reading, writing, and drawing. Collect old cushions and rugs to make it cozy, and hang mats from the roof to give privacy. Create a retreat that will make you long to be a castaway on your imaginary desert island.

MATERIALS NEEDED FOR
DESERT ISLAND LODGE

In addition to materials listed for **The Basic Platform** *(see page 44)*, you will also require:

1 wall board: ¾ inch x 2 x 8 feet
1 wall board: ¾ inch x 2 x 4 feet
6 roof supports: 1 x 2 inches x 4 feet
2 spacers for wall/post: 1 x 2 x 24 inches
4 or 5 bannisters: 1 x 2 x 24 inches
3 long rails: 1 x 2 inches x 8 feet
3 short rails: 1 x 2 inches x 51 inches
Exterior varnish or paint

ROOF
Bamboo screen
Wooden roof (optional): ¾ inch x 4 x 8-foot board and additional 1 x 2 inches x 4 feet posts to replace some of the bannisters

FASTENERS
4 screws or bolts: 4 inches long
Screws: 2–2¾ inches, assorted

PREPARATION

Cut all wood in advance. This structure consists of four walls added to the basic platform. Two are solid board and two are made from rails. In addition, there are four corner posts that will support a roof. The height of the walls that you use is up to you. We have used a height of 24 inches because it is economical to cut a 4-foot standard board down the center. Whatever height you choose you can adjust the 24-inch dimensions to suit.

CONSTRUCTING THE LADDER

Choose the strongest wood that you have available. First, make a mark on the ground directly below where the ladder is to be attached. Measure that height and quarter it, then mark that new measurement out from the first mark, away from the tree house. Take the distance from the new mark to the fastening points on the platform and cut two pieces of 2 x 2s at least 8 inches longer (to allow for attaching and hand rail).

Decide upon a width for your ladder (about 18 inches should be fine) and cut enough lengths of 1 x 2s to make a rung every 12 inches up the ladder. If you are confident that you

crews will be good and tight, use two screws at each end to attach the rungs to the ladder posts. Use two pieces of wood cut to 10 inches as temporary spacers to get the rungs even. If you are concerned about your screw fastenings, add pieces of wood between the rungs as permanent spacers.

Attach the ladder to the platform using long substantial screws or bolts. Sharpen two stakes of 2 x 2s and drive them into the ground on both sides of the ladder. Attach the ladder to these with screws.

TO FIT THE WALLS

Starting at the short end of the platform, take the 48-inch length of board and position it to cover the end beam. Attach it with pairs of screws placed every 6 inches. Do the same with the longer 8-foot piece of board along the back edge of the platform.

Take one of the spacers and place it in the corner created by the two boards. Screw both boards firmly to the post using screws spaced about 6 inches apart.

Screw four roof supports to the substantial wood of the beams at the corners of the platform on its long side (they should extend 4 inches below the platform surface). Two posts must be fitted outside of the long wall board (screw the rest of the board to it). Another post will need the second spacer strip so you can attach the short board to it. Screw the bannisters and the remaining two roof supports to the substantial platform

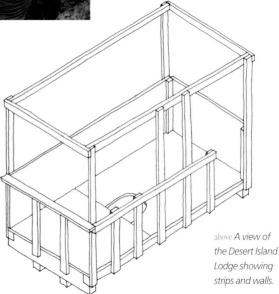

above A view of the Desert Island Lodge showing strips and walls.

beams so that the bannisters' tops are level. Spread them out evenly along the open sides of the tree house with the two roof supports along the center of the long side.

Attach the rails across the corner posts at bannister height. If you want to make a wider rail along the short edge to put things on, fit the rail flipped sideways so you can screw down through the rail into the bannister tops. Cut away the rail where you want the entrance to be. Screw the roof rails to the tops of the roof supports, being careful while working up high.

ADDING THE ROOF

There are a variety of ways of dealing with the roof, depending on how much foliage you will have to work around at that height. The simplest way is to use a roll of bamboo screen or matt, as would suit a retreat on an exotic desert island. It can be easily cut to fit around small branches and over twigs. Alternatively, you can use planks, bamboo, or cut branches to build up a roof covering, arranging these around any awkward branches. If you want a more solid roof, a thin 4 x 8-foot board can be used. Fit it using the same technique described for adding the platform board. Because a board roof will be heavy and catch the wind, you must strengthen the rails and screw it down firmly. Replace some of the bannisters with full-length posts and add several wood strips across the roof structure.

THE FINISHING TOUCHES

You have now made the basic tree house. All that remains is to finish off the details. First, be careful of any wood that protrudes or looks out of place. Next, you should weatherproof the tree house by painting it with exterior-quality varnish or fence paint. If you don't want a paint finish, at least seal the exposed parts of the tree house that are structural or made from board. Use varnish if avoiding a painted appearance, or a light-colored paint which will give a look appropriate to a sun-bleached tropical tree house.

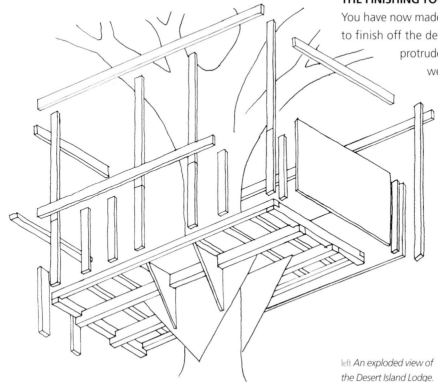

left *An exploded view of the Desert Island Lodge.*

PIRATE SHIP

Like the previous tree house, this structure is based on the Basic Platform described at the beginning of this section. It looks complex but is not much more difficult to build than the Desert Island Lodge. The main innovation used for this tree house is the hull shape beneath the main platform. This doesn't require any clever joints or complex cutting;

instead, the hull is built up of overlapping slats like a fence. These slats need to be at least long enough to span three ribs of the ship's hull, or you will have problems attaching them. Find them by dismantling lap fence panels or cut thin board into strips.

Or, try your local lumberyard for scraps of sapwood trimmings, or thin, flexible planks.

MATERIALS NEEDED FOR
PIRATE SHIP

In addition to materials listed for The Basic Platform *(see page 44),* you will also require:

1 board for cutting hull supports: ¾ inch x 4 x 8 feet
2 prow beams: 2 x 4 x 4 inches or longer
thin slats for paneling the hull: about 110 square feet, equivalent to two 6-foot fence panels
1 back wall of cabin: ¾ x 24 x 48-inch board
2 side walls of cabin: ¾ x 24 x 48-inch board
2 spacing strips: 1 x 2 x 20 inches
4 roof support posts: 2 x 2 x 60 inches
4 roof support strips: 1 x 2 x 48 inches
1 roof board: 4 x 4 feet
4 rail posts: 1 x 2 x 24 inches
A large branch
Exterior varnish/paint

FASTENERS
Screws: 2–2¾ inches, assorted
Nails for slats
Polypropylene rope or wire

(CUTTING PLAN: PAGE 148)

PREPARATION

Cut all the wood pieces in advance. Before you begin building, look at the cutting plan for the hull *(see page 148)*. It shows a series of curved supports that will be used to attach the hull paneling. There is one for four of the six crossbeams on the platform and one for each end beam (the center supports, D and E, are part of the basic platform). It may look complicated but you will get all the shapes needed out of one board. The shapes are all nested together. This plan will save you a lot of work because each cut will shape two components.

Once you have marked the board, cut along all the lines using a saber saw. Be sure to mark the identifying letters on each piece before you forget its place in the order.

AT THE TREE

At the platform, decide which direction you want the ship to face. At the front of the ship, cut two holes through the platform next to the main supports. These must be large enough to pass a length of 2 x 4 beam through. Find two long scraps of 2 x 4s, which must be the same length. Pass these two prow beams through the holes and screw them to the supporting beams at the angle that you want to achieve for the ship's prow.

Next, make a series of ribs, which the hull boards will be curved over. These do not have to be perfectly aligned because the hull wood will average out any discrepancies. Starting at the front of the ship, mark each crossbeam with a letter in sequence from A to H (including both end beams). From the hull supports that you cut previously, take the one marked A and screw this to the center of the end beam so that it hangs downward. Take the next hull support in the series (marked B) and screw this to the side of the next crossbeam, also marked B. Continue in this way until you have attached support H to the beam at the end of the platform. You will notice that supports D and E are already in place—you attached them when you made the platform. If any of the curved supports don't fit, hold them up and mark what needs to be removed, then trim the wood so that they do.

TRANSFERRING THE CUTTING PLAN TO YOUR BOARD

First, draw the same background grid onto your board, then mark all the measurement points. Copy the curves over one at a time, all the while checking where each curve crosses the background grid. If it crosses a grid-line about halfway across a box, make yours do the same.

Constantly check to ensure it looks correct relative to any other curves and don't be afraid to correct any lines after you have made them..

1. Adding the prow beams through the platform board.

2. Cutting the curved hull frames.

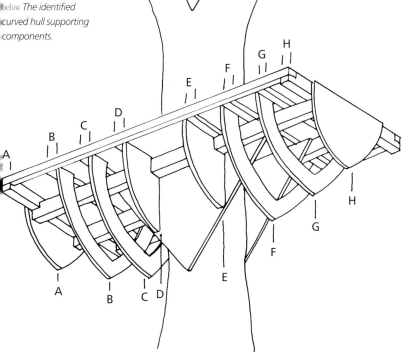

below The identified curved hull supporting components.

PIRATE SHIP

1. *Attaching the curved hull supports.*

2. *Securing the slats to the hull.*

PANELING THE HULL

To panel the completed ribs you will need some thin, flexible planks. They do not need to be strong or even straight—we've used the slats from sections of prefabricated lap fence panels.

Add the slats to the hull, starting from the bottom. Take one slat and, using annular ring nails, nail it to each rib as you pull it to fit around the form. When a slat will not reach the next rib, leave it and nail another one to overlap it, starting at the last rib to which you are able to nail. When you reach the end of the hull, leave any overhang to be cut off when the paneling is finished. Continue adding slats, working upward, and slightly overlap each band until you reach the platform. Be careful that the paneling does not overlap the platform's edges.

When the whole hull is paneled, finish the stern of the ship first. Take an extra slat that will fit vertically over the attached slats so that it covers the stern rib. Nail it firmly in place to stop the other slats from springing off in the future. Trim off all the slats that overhang the rear of the ship. At the front of the ship, trim the overlapping slats where they want to cross each other.

The line that they make should continue the line of the keel up to the point of the prow. It may take a few attempts to get the line looking right, but you can always add new slats to improve the shape. Once you are satisfied with the curve at the prow drill two holes through the end of the top slats on each side of the boat. Use these holes to tie the slats together on both sides with wire or polyurethene rope.

ADDING THE SUPERSTRUCTURE

The cabin walls are made from three pieces of board: one that spans the back of the ship and two that cover the sides. The side walls are shaped to resemble the scrollwork of a galleon's poop deck. Transfer the cutting plan (*see page 148*) for the side walls in the same way as you did the hull ribs and cut them both out with a saber saw. Save the scraps, which can be used as decorative scrolls for dressing the ship.

Screw the 24 x 48-inch back wall to the solid beam at the rear of the ship and then screw strips to its edges. Add the first side wall, tilting it downward to follow the curve of the hull.

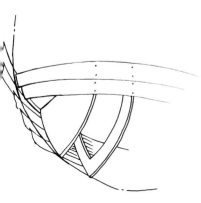

3. *Marking the decorative scrolls for the side walls.*

left *Finding the line of the prow at the front of the ship to trim the slats to.*

RAIL SAFETY ALERT!

When attaching rails to a platform, make sure that they are firmly secured. Use screws or bolts that go deep into the wood to which you are attaching. Check the secured rails to make sure that they are strong enough, and strengthen them, if necessary. Having no rail at all could be safer than giving false confidence in a rail that will break if someone leans on it.

Make sure that it overlaps the edge of the back wall. Screw it in place at the supporting platform beams and to the strips you have just added to the back wall. Add the other side wall in the same way, attempting to get a matching tilt.

Attach the roof support posts to the side walls: one at the front and one at the rear of each side wall. Use the spacers to support the rear posts. To support the roof, add the cross members to link the tops of all the roof posts. For the roof, either use a rectangle of board that is firmly screwed down or an alternative like those used for the previous tree house. Screw a rail post securely to the platform base at each crossbeam. The tops of these rail posts have rope tied across them to act as a safety rail. Ropes can be attached by nailing a staple into the top of the posts or by drilling a hole and threading the rope through. Wrap the rope around the posts and perhaps across the rails.

Add a ladder as described in the previous project. Then you can turn your attention to adding decorative detail, and allow your imagination to sail the high seas.

FINISHING OFF THE WOODWORK

Add a bowsprit to the prow of the ship using the two posts added at the start of this section. As the ship has a tree for a mast, the bowsprit can be made from a branch. Find one that is substantial enough to look good at the front of the ship; then use several long screws or bolts to attach it to the prow posts so that it overhangs at a convincing angle. The ropes that connect the rails can be extended to join this branch.

Use the scraps from the side walls and the curved supports for decorating the cabin. The rear of the cabin is a good place for decoration: aim for it to resemble the scrolls at the rear of a galleon. You can cut portholes in the walls by drilling a hole large enough to insert a saber-saw blade and cutting out a disk (use the disk elsewhere for decoration). If you want, add a rudder using a strip of board long enough to span from above the rear wall to below the hull. Cut it into a rudder shape and attach it to the outside of the rear wall using two hinges. Attach a hand pole to the top of the rudder to steer the ship from inside.

PIRATE SHIP

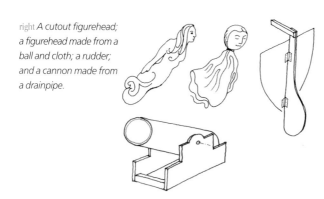

right *A cutout figurehead; a figurehead made from a ball and cloth; a rudder; and a cannon made from a drainpipe.*

PAINTING AND DECORATING

You should paint the tree house to protect it from the rain, especially the parts made from board. Use exterior-quality varnish or fence paint for a uniform color. Use colorful interior paint to add decoration and detail, such as the ship's name.

No ship is complete without a figurehead, and there are many ways of making one to suit your ship. Draw the profile of a figure onto a piece of board and cut around it, then screw into place. Alternatively, try the scarecrow approach by wrapping a ball in cloth for the head and adding clothing, twigs, and straw or binding and stuffing. A soft toy or doll can make a familiar figurehead (be sure not to forget it and leave it outside).

Of course, the ship will need rigging and perhaps sails. You can attach rope to the platform from branches farther up the tree. Add some staples or blocks of wood to tie the rope to, if needed. Sails can be hoisted up these ropes. A flagpole with a painted skull and crossbones adds authenticity.

You can make a ship's wheel by using cut board or a suitable round object, such as a bicycle wheel. Screw it directly to the tree trunk, adding a block of wood with a hole drilled in it, to keep the wheel spaced away from the tree.

right *An exploded view of the Pirate Ship's basic components, not showing the rope rails or rigging.*

FINAL DRESSING IDEAS

A cannon can be made from a length of plastic drain pipe bolted to a simple wooden base or even a box.

Cut an anchor from a board or assemble one from scrap strips; tie it to the prow with string.

Nets and plastic lobsters can complete the nautical feeling of the ship, as can a telescope, bandanas, and eye patches.

Platform Variation

The following two tree houses, the Windmill and the Lighthouse, are built on a variation of the single, straight-trunk platform that was used for the previous two tree houses. The main difference in construction of the platform is that it uses ground braces instead of the triangular braces we saw before. The basic technique of bolting a pair of supporting beams to the trunk remains the same.

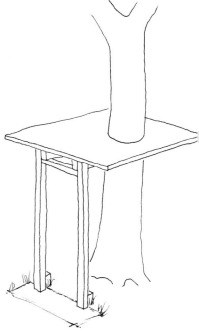

MATERIALS NEEDED FOR
PLATFORM VARIATION

Additional materials required for each project are listed on the relevant pages. For this Platform Variation, you will require:

2 support beams: 2 x 4 x 48 inches
2 stakes: 2 x 2 x 4 inches (sharpened)
2 wood strips: 2 x 2 inches x 6½ feet or longer if the
    ground slopes
1 door spacer wood strip: 2 x 2 x 24 inches
2 small triangles of plywood
Platform board: ¾ inch x 4 x 4 feet, left square for the
    Windmill, cut to a 48-inch-diameter circle for the Lighthouse

FOR THE SUPPORTING WALLS
4 curved supports: 24-inch radius, ¾-inch board
4 panel strips: 1 x 2 inches x 5 feet 10½ inches
4 plywood panel faces: ⅛ inch x 38 inch x 6-foot board
2 wall posts: 1 x 2 inches x 6½ feet
6 or more flat stone/cement slabs

FASTENERS
2 screw bolts: ⅜-inch diameter, 6–8 inches long, with washers
4 bolts: ⅜-inch diameter, 4¾ inches long, each with a pair of
    washers and nuts
Screws: 2–3¾ inches, assorted
Twisted nails

(CUTTING PLAN, PAGE 149)

THE PLATFORM

Mark up the tree in the same way as the previous section, only this time make the height of the platform 6 feet from the highest ground. Ensure that the bolt marks are level. Decide what direction you want the tree house to face.

Measure the maximum width of the trunk at the approximate height of the platform and generously round this measurement up to the nearest 4 inches (a 16½-inch trunk becomes 20 inches). Take two 4-foot-long, 2 x 4 beams and mark from one end the equivalent of half the tree trunk width (e.g. for a 20-inch trunk width, measure 10 inches), this will mark the bolt holes. Drill them so the bolt can pass through

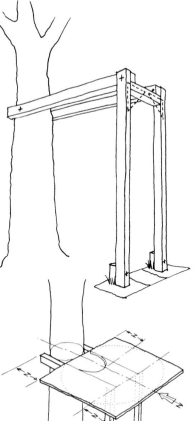

1. Setting out the upright support to the first main beam.

2. Positioning the second upright support.

3. Attaching the upright to the stake.

left *The main beams and upright supports with the "doorway" spacer, stakes, and footing slabs.*

left *Marking the platform board for the trunk cutout.*

Drill pilot holes at the bolt marks on the tree and, with their length toward the front, bolt both beams (with washers) loosely to the tree so that they can be pivoted easily.

Get an assistant to hold one beam out toward the front so that it is level (check it with a level) and tighten up the bolts. While the beam is level, use a plumb bob to mark the spot on the ground directly below the end of the beam. Hammer a 2 x 2 stake firmly into the ground at this point. Hold a 6½-foot length of 2 x 2 up vertically from next to the stake and get the beam level against it. Mark where the top of the beam crosses the upright strip. Cut the strip to that length (if your tree house is on a slope, you might need a longer strip.) Attach the strip to the beam (on the opposite side to the tree) and to the stake, with a single bolt at each joint.

THE DOORWAY

Cut a wood strip to 24 inches and label it "doorway." Repeat the fitting of the upright for the second beam but this time use the "doorway" strip as a ruler to make sure that the upright is the same distance apart from the first upright.

Take the "doorway" strip and join both beams by screwing the strip beneath the two beams where the uprights meet them. Make sure that the posts are upright and parallel and that the doorway looks straight. Screw the two small triangles to the top corners of the doorway using at least three screws on each side.

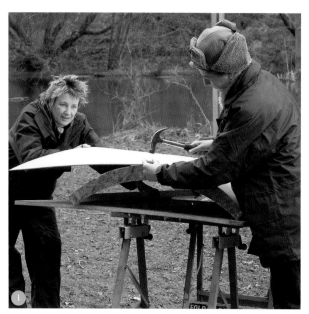

1. *Adding the plywood face to the wall panels.*

below *An exploded view of one wall panel.*

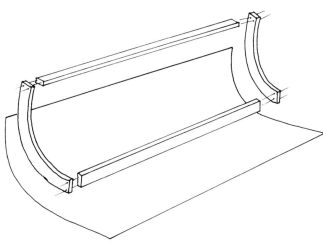

THE PLATFORM FLOOR

Take a 4 x 4-foot square board and slide it onto the beams until it touches the tree, making sure that the doorway is centered at the front. Cut a hole in the board to accommodate the tree as described in the previous section (*see page 50*). Once it is cut, slide the board into position to check that it fits flush with the doorway and the doorway is centered. Do not screw it down.

IMPORTANT: If you are making the Lighthouse, cut the platform board into a circle with a 24-inch radius (*see the panel on drawing circles on page 73*) before you continue. For the Windmill, leave the platform as a square.

WALLS

To make the curved supporting walls, cut a pair of curved supports from board as shown on the cutting plan. Screw a 5-foot-10½-inch-long, 1 x 2 wood strip to each end of one curved support. Join the other ends of the strip to another curved support, so that you have a curved frame. Attach a piece of ⅛-inch plywood that is 6 feet wide along one of the strips using annular ring nails. Then slowly bend the board around the curve, making sure its edge runs along the curved support, and securing it four or five times as you work. When you reach the other end, secure it along the other strip as before. You will need two of these curved supporting walls.

FASTENING

Place a curved supporting wall under the board platform so that it touches the door post and its other end is flush with the side edge of the platform. Use pieces of scrap wood to hold up the wall until it just presses on the underside of the platform board, then screw it onto the platform and the door frame. Position the one on the other side of the door in the same way.

At the end of each wall, measure from the platform to the ground and cut a wood strip ¾ inch longer to support the wall. Force it under the platform board and into the ground so that it is against the end strip in the curved wall. Make sure it is flush with the wall, and screw it on.

64

2. *Securing a wall panel to the underside of the platform.*

below *An exploded view showing the wall panels below the platform.*

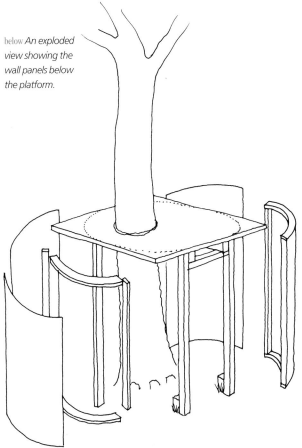

Starting at each of the new forced-in strips and ending behind the tree, add another piece of plywood and secure it over the gap from the outside. Join any overlapping plywood to the forced-in strips. The platform should now be very sturdy. If not, you can supplement the strength of the tree house by sliding bricks or flat stone slabs under the curved walls.

Now cut an opening in the platform board to allow for access from inside. Keep in mind that the doorway can be a potential hazard if it is placed in the center of the floor. A good place for it is alongside the tree. Mark an outline and cut it away, using a saber saw. To make the ladder, see pages 52–53.

RESTING POSTS ON THE GROUND

When resting posts on the ground, prepare the ground first. Clear away soft topsoil and, if possible, place a wide, flat stone to take the weight. Stakes will last longer if they are charred so that they have a carbonized surface.

PLATFORM VARIATION

WINDMILL

The Windmill uses a square platform over a rounded lower half as made for the Platform Variation. It has two floors, and, although it doesn't have an open deck, there is plenty of scope for adding windows. It can be built without a roof and with low walls to let the occupants be seen and to keep a sense of the outdoors;

or built with half a roof to give a balcony. The advantage of a roof is that it will give shelter on rainy days, as well as create a warmer space to play in. This structure can be built mostly on the ground (or in the garage), in advance and then assembled quickly. It's a great project to work on and develop over several weeks.

MATERIALS NEEDED FOR
WINDMILL

In addition to materials listed for the Platform Variation *(see page 62)*, you will also require:

2 pointed walls: ½ inch x 4 x 5-foot board, cut to plan
2 side walls: ½ inch x 3 x 4-foot board
4 wall strips: 2 x 2 x 34 inches
4 eaves strips: 2 x 2 inches x 2½ feet
2 base strips: 2 x 2 x 47 inches
2 base strips: 2 x 2 x 44 inches
1 ridge beam (optional): 2 x 2 x 47 inches
Roof covering (optional): two 3 x 4-foot panels, ⅜-inch board or planks
2 doorway planks: ¾ x 4¾ inches x 6 feet
1 doorway plank: ¾ x 4¾ x 33 inches
Additional wood required for shutters/window boxes
Exterior varnish/paint

FOR THE SAILS
4 spars: about 1 inch x 2 inch x 6 feet
28–44 wood strips (7–11 per sail): 1 x 2 x 18 inches

FASTENERS
Screws: ¾–4 inches, assorted

(CUTTING PLAN, PAGE 149)

PREPARATION

Prepare by cutting all wood in advance. The first thing to make is the facade of the Windmill. It consists of a single board cut to shape, with windows. The front and the back of the Windmill are exactly the same shape. If you don't want to add a roof, make the walls 12 inches lower. Check the tree to see if you have enough height for the roof; if not, you can always make the pitch more shallow.

Take two standard boards and transfer the cutting plan (*see page 149*). Cut out both of the pointed walls and side wall. Trim 1 inch off one short edge of each side wall. Also mark the bottom of the side walls. Decide where you want the windows, and cut them out.

Cut four 2 x 2s that are 1½ inches shorter than the height of the side walls. Screw two of these strips to each side wall so that one runs up each short edge. Make sure that they end 1½ inches short of the bottom edge. Cut two 2 x 2s that are 4 inches shorter than the diagonal edges. Screw these to the diagonal edges, making sure that they stop 2¼ inches from the point (the gap can be used for the roof ridge at the apex

1. *Cutting out the wall panel.*

2. *Adding the walls.*

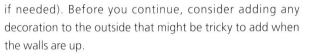

if needed). Before you continue, consider adding any decoration to the outside that might be tricky to add when the walls are up.

NEAT SABER SAW CUTS

The most untidy side of the cut is the side of the wood facing you, because the blade cuts on the upward stroke. Remember this and try to always cut out shapes from the back (the side that won't be seen).

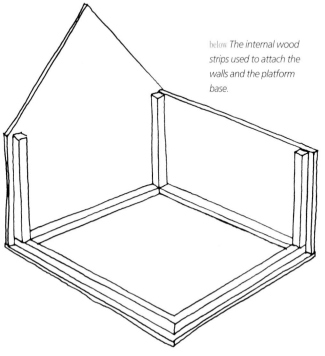

below *The internal wood strips used to attach the walls and the platform base.*

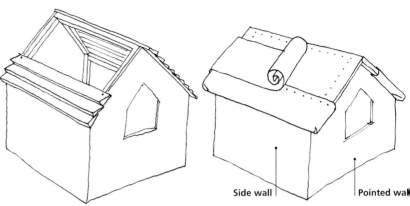

right *Various roof treatments are possible, the simplest and quickest being a roof made cut from a single board.*

below *The super-structure with the tree removed to show roof support principals.*

Side wall | **Pointed wall**

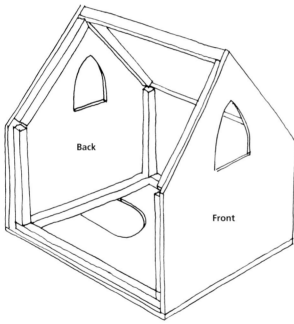

Back

Front

TEMPORARY FASTENING

If you are unsure if something will fit or if it is in the right place, use just a single screw or a clamp to hold it temporarily and try the next task in the building sequence to see if it works. Don't forget to secure it properly when you know that it's correct.

AT THE TREE

Mark a line around the edge of the platform, making a border the same thickness as the boards you will use for the walls. Use a scrap piece of board pressed against the edge to give you an accurate thickness. Cut two 2 x 2s to the length inside the border lines and place these strips on the line so they are set back from the edge—the distance from the edge being the thickness of the board. Attach the 2 x 2s by putting four screws up through the platform into them. Cut two more 2 x 2s that fit between the ends of the last strips, again within the border, and secure them in the same way.

Send an assistant up onto the platform and pass the front pointed wall up to him or her. Set the wall so that it rests in the border you marked on the platform, up against the strip. Check it is not overhanging either end and secure it with screws, using pilot holes.

Pass up each side wall in turn. Fit them flush to the edge of the pointed wall and screw them together. Run screws along the base as well. Finally, add the rear wall in a similar manner. If any of the wall panels won't fit because the tree is in the way, estimate what wood you will need to remove and cut it away—it may take several attempts. If you find that you have removed far too much, make a patch panel and screw it into place. Be careful that screws don't protrude inside.

1. *Making the sails, using a wood strip to ensure that the spacing is even.*

2. *Attaching the sails together.*

3. *Adding the sail assembly to a strip attached to the wall.*

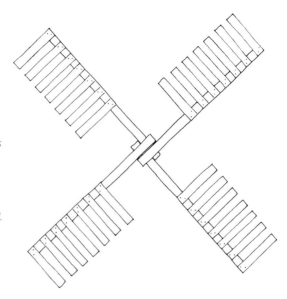

above The sails, *showing the strips overlapping at the center.*

FINISHING OFF

To make the top of the walls more substantial, screw a wood strip to the top edge of the board. If you intend to add a roof, now is a good time to do it. Cut a 2 x 2 to act as the roof ridge that fits between the apex of each pointed wall. Rest it in the notch between the strips that are secured along the roof edges. Either cut two boards to screw to the strips and roof ridge, or add a few extra strips running across the roof to which you can attach clapboards or even light wooden tiles.

The sails of the Windmill are made from four 1 x 2s screwed together at the ends to make a cross. Additional strips are screwed across them to make the vanes. It is important that the sails do not catch the wind efficiently because it will put a heavy load on the structure. Once constructed, the sails are bolted through a wood strip attached to the front wall.

The doorway of the Windmill should be finished with a door frame, consisting of two vertical planks and one horizontal plank nailed to the supporting posts. The door frame could be made to resemble a cottage door or a classical portal by shaping it with a saber saw, adding small cutout details and painting on designs. A light door can be added with hinges.

To decorate the windows, consider adding shutters cut from board, or window boxes with cutout flowers. Mutins can be imitated by tacking slats or cord diagonally across the window.

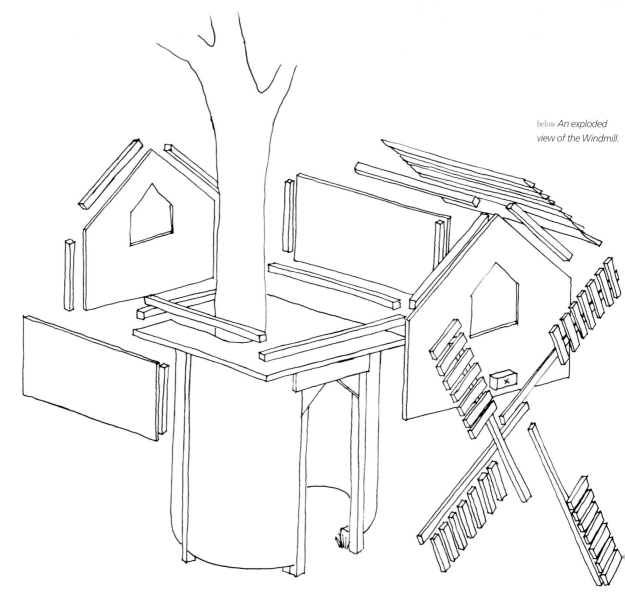

below An exploded view of the Windmill.

PAINTING AND DECORATING

The Windmill should be painted to protect it from the effects of the weather. An exterior varnish should be applied to all board used in its construction. Or colored fence paint can be used to seal the wood. Paint on mock wooden paneling or brickwork, or train a climbing rose around the doorway. Decorative ivy could be encouraged to ramble over the whole structure.

There is plenty of scope to decorate the site of the Windmill. You can simulate a rural idyll by running a small, white picket fence around it. Try casually arranging some flour sacks (burlap sandbags stuffed with straw) or even planting some corn around the base. Potted bay trees, cart wheels, and, of course, tulips, will make for an authentic atmosphere. You can also add milk churns or anything your imagination conjures.

1. *Stringing the Lighthouse "window panes" using plastic rope for durability.*

far right *The threading route for the plastic rope.*

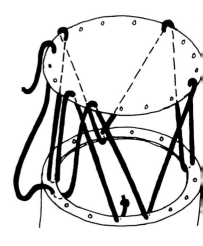

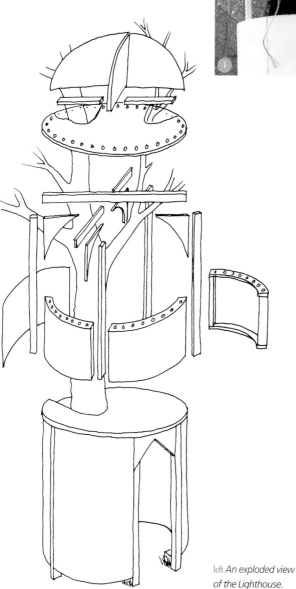

left *An exploded view of the Lighthouse.*

THE FINISHING TOUCHES

To complete the lantern at the top of the tree house, take some rope or cord and lace it through the holes in the curved wall, following the diagram above.

To construct the dome for the Lighthouse, take the two semicircular intersectors you cut out earlier and slot them together. Position this domed structure on the top of the roof and attach it securely using screws and four short wood strips.

Make a suitable doorway for the Lighthouse in the same way as described for the Windmill.

PAINTING AND DECORATING

As with all wooden tree houses, you should protect the structure from the weather. Use either exterior varnish to seal the wood, or fence paint to seal and add color. Textured house paint is ideal for the Lighthouse.

Lighthouses are often painted with red-and-white horizontal stripes, but this is your Lighthouse, so you get to choose the colors you prefer. If you feel that bright color would ruin the look of your yard, you can consider painting the Lighthouse with a stone-block effect.

You can add rocks to the base of the Lighthouse—either real ones, cutouts made of wood, or simply painted ones. Essential additions are a bright flashlight to warn ships that gets too close, a foghorn, and a telescope. Other accessories might include a parrot or seagull, a wrecked boat, a whale's skeleton, or some circling sharks—use your ingenuity.

TREE HOUSES
FOR TREES WITH FORKED TRUNKS

INTRODUCTION

Sometimes a tree looks as though it were just waiting to have a tree house built in it. Some even have crowns of branches that look as though you could easily occupy them without building any structure. Often, these are the best trees to build in, with the branches themselves suggesting the form of the tree house. As tempting as it may be to simply nail

some wood to the branches and make it up as you go, it is safer to plan the structure and fastenings first. Adding planks and boards ad hoc may damage the tree and risk collapse of the platform. In this section, we look at forked trees and how to work with an extra branch on forked trees. The last example in this section explores an entirely different method for

78

PLATFORM CONSIDERATIONS

Trees that have a significant fork or substantial branch are most commonly used for tree houses, often because the shapes they make suggest the possibility of a structure for building. These "ideal" trees come in two varieties. The first is where one or more substantial branches leave the trunk at a similar level, creating a crown or natural platform. The other is where a trunk forks on its way upward and provides two firm main branches within which to build.

When planning a tree house in these types of trees, you have the benefit of several distant fastening points, a major advantage over a single trunk. You can also take advantage of the strength of the tree to extend the tree house farther out.

When planning the fastenings for this type of tree, it is important to remember that the tree will move in the wind. It is this ability to bend and move that let the tree survive even high gusts. Your tree house will benefit by following the example of the tree, one of accepting movement and flexing with it.

The solution to all this movement is to use fastenings that can rotate and beams that can slide. On top of this, you build a sturdy platform that isn't attached directly to any trunks or branches. You must be careful not to join two trunks together with a secured beam, unless it is at the same level as the trunk's fork or where a main branch forks out from the trunk.

SLIDING SUPPORTS

For your first project, you will build a basic platform on a tree that has two uprights; either a trunk and a main branch or a forked trunk. This platform can be built on a fork in a tree or in a tree with a natural platform. A variation on this platform shows how it can be easily adapted to fit a tree with more branches or a more complex natural crown.

The main feature of this design is that each main beam will be supported at both ends; one end secured with a bolt, the other resting on a support that will let it slide.

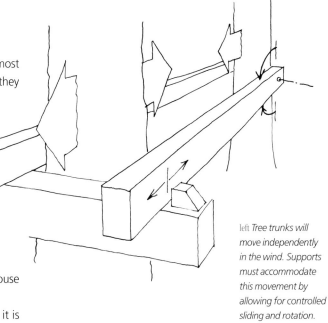

left Tree trunks will move independently in the wind. Supports must accommodate this movement by allowing for controlled sliding and rotation.

MOVING FASTENINGS AND SLIDING

Whenever a structure joins across two separate trunks, it will be subject to the stresses imposed by the independent movement of the two trunks as their branches move in the wind. These stresses are large and can severely damage the fastenings and possibly the structure itself.

To avoid the risk of your fasteners failing, take the movement into account and allow for it to happen in a controlled way. To do this, provide a location where the spanning beam can slide over a support. This sliding movement must be limited to a single direction—the same one that the trunks will move in—and, apart from this allowed movement, the beam must be restrained in all other directions.

Ways of doing this include making special steel runners or resting a beam in a channel on another secured beam so that it can slide along its length. Side blocks and end-stop blocks should be used to limit any sideways movement and to stop the beam from sliding right out of its groove.

MOVING BRANCHES

If you consider how branches move, you will understand that there is less movement at the point where the branches meet—at a fork for example—than there is higher up the branches, where they behave almost separately in relation to each other.

When your fastening point is close to a fork, you can assume that there will be little movement. Conversely, there will be a great deal of force in what movement there is.

Farther up the branches there is no way of predicting how much movement there will be, so we have to assume it can go in many directions, throughout a circular zone.

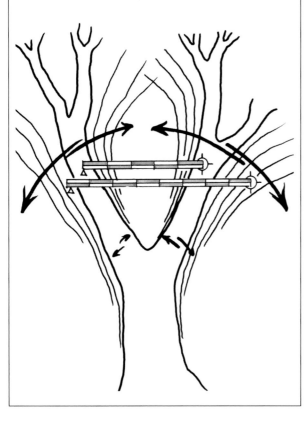

CHOOSING A FORKED TREE

The ideal tree for this platform is one that has two obvious upright main branches. It doesn't matter whether one is the main trunk or not, provided that they are both reasonably thick. Check to be sure that there are no splits where the two branches meet and that there is no danger of one of the branches falling off in the future. It does not matter if the two branches are of different thicknesses.

The two branches should be far enough apart so that there is a useful area between them, because this is where the platform will be. We used trees that are 40 to 100 inches apart. If the branches are farther apart, you will need to increase the length of the support beams. If the distance is much more, you may also need to increase the thickness and depth of the beams, otherwise they will sag and be springy to walk on—which can be unnerving in a tree house.

IRREGULARITIES AND DEAD BRANCHES

Locate an even and parallel stretch of trunk on each branch, level with each other. These are where your fastening points will go. If there are any large bumps or growths, try moving up or down a bit on both branches. Any minor irregularities can be sawn off, keeping in mind that you should not damage live bark. If any branches or twigs will be in the way, you should cut off just the minimum amount necessary.

Don't write off potential branches that are obviously dead—they can still provide a strong fastening point. In fact, they offer even better potential for the tree house because you can cut, nail, and screw into them without harming the tree. You might consider cutting flat faces into the side of a dead branch to create good fastening points, or cutting the branch off level to provide a sound support or a useful small platform. Be sure to check any dead wood for strength before deciding to use it. Push a screwdriver into the wood or drill a small hole—if it is soft, the wood is weak. Also check a dead bough for splits or hollows. Only build onto thick, strong wood that is obviously well attached to the tree.

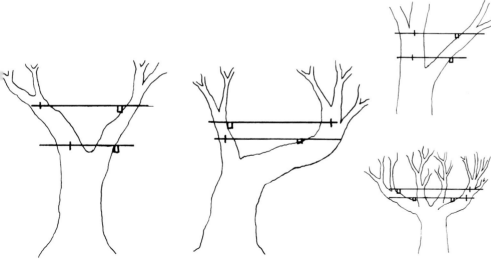

left Different fastening possibilities for bolts and beams on various levels of a forked tree.

below A large tree like this offers a world of possibilities but also a great deal of different challenges to consider.

WIRE ROPE AND FASTENERS

Wire rope is easy to use once you are familiar with its fittings. The wire rope itself is always used with a loop at both ends, and to this you can attach all kinds of useful fittings, such as tensioners and swivels.

To make a loop, you must allow for enough cable to be doubled back upon itself so that you can attach at least three wire rope clips across the overlapped lengths of wire. Inside the loop you should place a small teardrop-shaped metal fitting called a thimble. This will keep the loop tidy and prevent it from wearing or breaking. It is usual to pinch the thimble tightly into the loop with the first wire rope clip so that it cannot slip out.

The other two clips are usually placed so that one is near the end of the overlap, the other midway between them. The clips must be the right size for the wire rope being used and each size of clip should be tightened to the torque setting that it is designed for. If you are in doubt, ask the supplier for advice.

Once you have the length of wire rope required with a loop at both ends, use shackles to connect to the loops of any other fittings or to the eyebolts that are attached to the load. Each assembly should include a tensioner so that you can make fine adjustments to the length and tension of the wire rope.

81

The Basic Platform

MATERIALS NEEDED FOR THE BASIC PLATFORM

Additional materials required for each project are listed on the relevant pages. For the Basic Platform, you will require:

1 platform board: ¾ inch x 4 x 8 feet
Additional board to fill gaps: ¾-inch board
2 main support beams: 2 x 4 x 48 inches
4 "branch-span" support beams:
    2 x 4 inches x branch-span length
    plus 40 inches
6 spacers: 2 x 4 inches x space between
    branch-span beams
8 end-stop blocks: 2 x 4 inches (optional)

FOR THE WIRE ROPE
4 eyebolts with nuts and washers
4 lengths of stainless steel wire rope
    of the correct thickness (see page 135)
8 wire rope thimbles
12 quick links or shackles
24 wire rope clamps
4 screw eyes
4 bottle tensioners

FOR THE LADDER
Posts: 2 x 2 inches x the length of the
    slope to the entrance
Rungs: 2 x 2 inches, number and length
    determined by ladder height and width
Flat slab or stone

FASTENERS
2 bolts: ½–¾-inch diameter, 8 inches
    long, with washers and spring washers
Screws: 2–2¾ inches, assorted

This platform and the tree-house structures that follow it have been made on two separate trees. The first is a symmetrical, evenly forked tree and the second a more quirkily formed, leaning tree. The basic principle is the same for setting a platform between any two branches. The various structures that we describe are for known platform-board dimensions. However, because the dimensions of the tree that you choose will be different, when we refer to the size of some support beams, it will be in terms of what they will need to span up until the point where the platform board, which has known dimensions, is fitted. You will need to measure your tree and find the support beam dimensions that are particular to it. You may want to combine several different types of platforms to create different levels for your tree house and the last variation includes an additional small, single-trunk platform. This is made in the way described in the previous section so it is not repeated in detail here.

left *The basic platform used for the Spooky Hideout and the Enchanted Castle rests on a bent trunk with a small, forking branch.*

1. *Leveling the first support.*

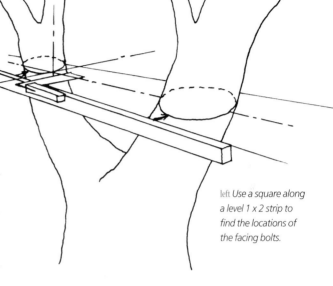

left *Use a square along a level 1 x 2 strip to find the locations of the facing bolts.*

MARKING THE TREE AND SETTING FASTENING POINTS

To set the height of your tree-house platform, stand back from the tree so that you can clearly see both of the upright branches and visualize where the platform will go. Look for two clear parallel stretches of branches roughly at the same level. Keep in mind that the platform will be approximately 4¼ inches thick, so any other branches or obstacles should be below your chosen location points by this much. Mark the level you have chosen onto one of the branches, using the top edge of a piece of tape to represent where you want the top of the platform to be.

Measure the overall distance between the two branches, including the branches themselves. We will refer to this distance as the "branch span." Get a 1 x 2 that is at least as long as the branch span and hold it up level with the top of the tape so that it touches the far branch. It will be useful to have an assistant to help you support the strip. Alternatively, you can use temporary nails to support the tape end.

Check that the 1 x 2 is still at the edge of the tape, and use a level to ensure it is lying perfectly horizontal to the other branch. Slide a square along the 1 x 2 until it touches the branch, and mark that point with the top tape edge. Go back and do the same at the first branch. You should now have two level fastening points that face each other across the branches.

PREPARING THE SUPPORT BEAMS

Cut two 2 x 4 main support beams to 48 inches long, and four 2 x 4 branch-span beams to 40 inches longer than the branch span (if the branch span is less than 100 inches, make the beams

11½ feet). Drill a ½-inch hole in the center of the 4-inch face of both support beams, then drill a ⅜-inch hole 4 inches in from each end of both beams.

ATTACHING THE FRAMEWORK TO THE TREE

Take the first support beam with a hole in the center and, using a pilot hole, bolt it to one of the branches at the level fastening point mark. Be sure to include washers at both sides of the beam and a spring washer under the head. Do the same at the other branch with the other support beam. Check each with a level and tighten completely. Attach a ⅜-inch-diameter eyebolt in the ⅜-inch hole at the ends of each support beam, using washers. The eyebolts must face toward the other branch.

Locate a point on both branches about 40 inches below each fastening point and screw in screw eyes. Attach each support-beam eyebolt to the screw eye below it, using wire rope and a tensioner. Tighten them evenly in turns until they ring when you pluck them. *(For attaching wire rope, see page 81.)*

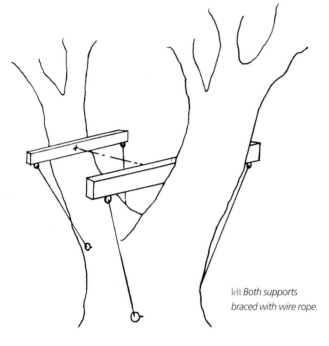

left *Both supports braced with wire rope.*

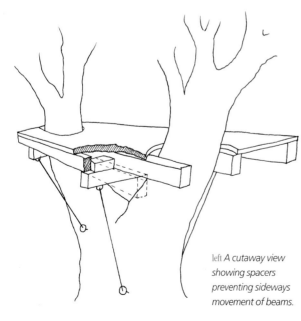

left *A cutaway view showing spacers preventing sideways movement of beams.*

Take one of the branch-span beams and rest it over both of the support beams so that it is 4 inches clear of each branch. Be sure that it overhangs the support beams by the same amount at each end. Use a screw to temporarily attach the beam by screwing upward through the support beam. Repeat this with a branch-span beam on the other side of the tree (4 inches clear), then place the remaining two branch-span beams at the extreme ends of the support beam. Ensure that the end of each branch-span beam overhangs the support beam by the same amount. The platform board will be secured to these beams, and when they have the temporary screws removed, they will be free to slide with the tree's movement.

Make six spacers to ensure the branch-span beams can only slide along their length. Measure and cut six pieces of 2 x 4 so that they fit on top of the support beam between the side beams. They must slide easily into position. Screw them firmly down on to the support beam using three long screws.

STRENGTHENING THE PLATFORM

This platform relies on the platform board to provide strength. It must be firmly screwed down to the branch-span beams to become rigid. If there is more than 8½ feet between the two branches, it will be a simple matter to lift up the platform board to rest on the branch-span beams. Leave the same gap between both branches and the ends of the board.

If the branches are spaced less than 8½ feet apart, it will be necessary to cut the board 8 inches shorter than the distance between the branches. Attach it on top of the branch-span beams so that there is 4 inches clearance at either end. Before you fasten the board down, make sure that the outside branch-span beams are flush with the edge of the board, then screw the board down securely to all the branch-span beams.

The final task is to fit board over the remaining exposed beams. If you are planning to build the Throne (the first tree house shown for this platform), it only uses a short platform so it will not be necessary to fit any more board around the tree.

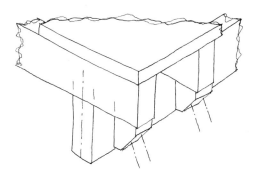

1. *Adding spacers between the branch-span beams.*

2. *The first section of platform board in place.*

3. *Adding the platform end boards.*

4. *The completed platform.*

below *End stops are attached to the bottoms of beams on shorter platforms.*

FINISHING OFF

We now have a board supported by four beams that protrude a long way past both the board and the branches of the tree. These branch-span beams need to be longer than the supports that they sit on or they would "derail" in a strong wind.

However, if you feel that the tree is fairly immobile and that stormy conditions will not flex the structure much, it might be possible to cut them shorter. They will need to extend beyond the main supports regardless. If in doubt, leave them long for a couple of windy spells and then check for evidence of wear.

Paint the bearing surfaces to show up any movement, or bang in a series of small nails that will be bent out of the way. The measure of wear will give you an idea of where it should be safe to cut. If you do cut them, add a strong block of wood to the underside of each beam end to act as an end stop.

A better option would be to take advantage of all that potential platform by adding an extra amount of board to the exposed beams. Measure from the end of the beams to the branch and subtract 4 inches to give the branch space to move, then cut this length from a board and screw it down flush with the ends of the beams. Do this at both ends of the tree-house platform. Finally, cut filler squares to bridge the gaps between the two beams at either side of the branch and secure them with screws.

This filling can be done by cutting a curved "bite" out of one piece of board, cut to the length of the remaining beams. If you try this, leave a 4-inch gap around the branch to allow for movement. Once the deck is fitted, remove the screws that you temporarily put up through the main supports into the branch-span beams. Slightly loosen the main support bolts, so that the spring washer can take up any sideways movement of the trunk.

THRONE

Sometimes the best thing that you can do in a tree house is to just sit and enjoy being up in the tree, above everyone else, monarch of all you survey. Although not strictly a tree house, this project will provide you with a throne worthy of your elevated position, or perhaps just a magical place to go and ponder life's complexities while taking in the view. *The Throne can be oversized compared to most chairs, with plenty of room for two or more people. Based on the forked-tree platform described in the previous section, it is a simple project. There is plenty of scope for additions and alterations.* Consider your tree to imagine what kind of throne would best suit your regal moments.

MATERIALS NEEDED FOR
THRONE

In addition to materials listed for the Basic Platform *(see page 82)*, you will also require:

2 back legs: 2 x 4 inches or thicker x 2.5 times the seat width
2 spacers: 2 x 4 inches x half the seat width
2 arms: 2 x 4 inches or thicker x the seat depth plus 12 inches
2 backrest supports: 2 x 2 inches x width of the seat
Backrest paneling: assorted possibilities, we have used 3 planks,
    1 x 6 inches x backrest height

FASTENERS:
4 screwbolts: ⅜-inch diameter, 8 inches long, with washers
Screws: 2–2¾ inches, assorted

PREPARATION

Prepare by cutting all wood in advance. Then, construct the forked tree basic platform described in the previous section. The platform board will act as your Throne's seat, so there is no need to go through the process of covering the exposed ends of the branch-span beams. Also consider reducing the length of the support beams so that they aren't longer than the front of the platform board; the seat will be best if it is square.

Much of the work for this platform can be carried out in advance. The arms, backrest, and back legs of the throne can be cut and partially assembled before the platform is even built, provided you know what size platform board you will be using. The front legs, which also act as the ladder for access, should only be made once you have the platform in place.

To give your throne the right proportions, the lengths of the various parts of the throne are based on the size of your platform board; we will call it the "seat." The upright posts that will be the back legs of the throne also continue straight up past the platform and become the side posts of the backrest. These back legs will be two-and-a-half times the seat width in length.

Cut two 2 x 4 posts to this length and then mark a line at the seat-width distance from each end. Each post will have two lines on it: one to align the platform, the other to align the armrests. Cut two pieces of 2 x 4s as spacers to fit between these marked lines, covering the midsection on both leg uprights. Screw them to the leg uprights face to face so that the wood now measures 4 inches x 4 inches at this central section.

For the arms, measure the depth of your platform seat plus 12 inches, then cut two pieces of 2 x 4s to this length. The backrest comprises of the two posts that you have already made, joined by the two backrest supports. These are then used to attach one of a variety of different backs. Make the backrest supports by cutting two 2 x 2s to the seat-width measurement that you used earlier for the back legs.

Now is a good time to decorate the main structure as you choose. Cut flourishes, carve wood, and use fretwork techniques if you want. Before doing this, you should run through the installation instructions until you are sure that you understand where the components go. Further ideas are supplied later, and decorating can also be done at the end of the project.

below Some sketched ideas for inspiration and decoration.

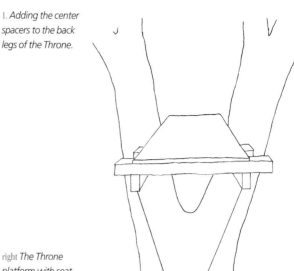

1. Adding the center spacers to the back legs of the Throne.

right The Throne platform with seat platform board fitted.

87

AT THE TREE

You will make the ladder first, which also serves as the front legs of the throne. To make the ladder more pleasant to climb, it is sloped slightly from the vertical.

Begin by selecting a firm patch of ground a short distance (about 20 inches for every 6½ feet height of the platform) in front of the tree directly forward of the platform. Position a flat slab of stone or concrete (or two flat slabs) so that it is about the same width as the seat, then draw a chalk line across the center of the slab so that it is parallel with the seat. Measure the distance from the platform down to the chalk line on the ground. You will need to cut two lengths of 2 x 4s that are this length, plus half of the seat depth, plus another 8 inches. You will need a rung for every foot of the ladder length, cut to the width of the seat platform. If you prefer a vertical ladder, just use the platform height measured straight down.

Once you have constructed the ladder, lean it against the seat so that the uprights extend beyond the platform and the base is on the slab. Get an assistant to hold the ladder while you climb up and attach the ladder to the base of the platform securely with screws. Take both of the back-leg assemblies and screw them to the rear of the platform. The bottom of the spacers should rest on the platform. Both the ladder and the back legs should be secured as firmly as possible to the beams of the platform.

The upper end of the spacer on the back leg is there to support the armrests, but before they can be fitted you will need to cut the protruding end of the ladder uprights to the same height. To do this, rest a level on the back-leg spacer and use it to mark a level line on the ladder upright. Then cut off the top from the upright along the line you have just drawn. Take both arms and rest them on the spacer and the ladder upright, and screw them down using several long screws at each location.

Next, you will need to attach the two backrest supports. These are used to secure your chosen backrest shape to. So that the backrest is comfortable to lean against, we will slope it slightly by fastening the lower support on the chair side of the backrests and the upper support on the outside of the backrest. Make sure they are completely securely attached by using at least two screws at each contact point.

The only thing that remains to be done is to attach the backrest. Whatever you choose to use, the basic principle is the same. Lean the backrest so that it touches both backrest supports and screw it to them. We have chosen to fit several planks for the backrest, and then cut the tops to make a pointed shape. To do this, you should begin by locating the central plank (leave it longer than will be needed) at the center of the backrest and screwing it down. Then add more planks one at time, leaving a slight gap, working outward until the space is filled. Finally, draw on the top profile and cut it out with the wood in situ.

FINISHING OFF

The main body of the throne is complete. Take a good look at it to make sure that nothing is out of place or poorly fastened. Go around sawing off any protruding ends of wood (remember not to remove the support beam sliders).

If you prefer, you can replace the ladder or just its rungs with a rope ladder, so that in the tree house you really are separated from the world.

For the back of the throne, you can use either slats or planks built up to make a surface or you can use board—perhaps with cutaway shapes, or a combination of both. Even woven branches or rope would work to create a particular style.

If you think you might spend some time up on your Throne, how about widening the armrests into small tables, or even adding a "lap" board? That way you could read or draw, and have a place to keep your royal refreshments.

1. *Measuring the distance from the platform to the chalk line.*

2. *The ladder in place before being trimmed to armrest level.*

3. *Attaching the backrest supports.*

4. *Cutting the tops of the backrest planks to form a point.*

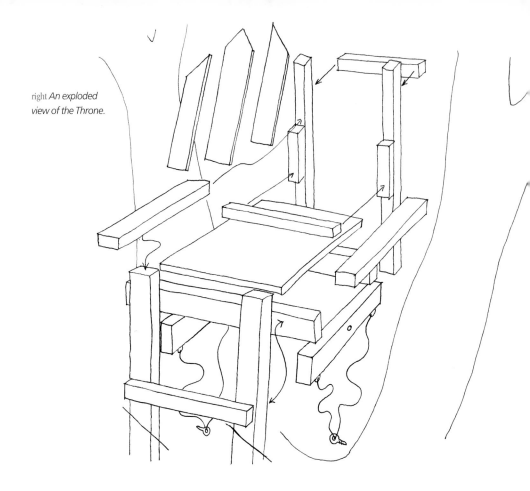

right *An exploded
view of the Throne.*

PAINTING AND DECORATING

There is plenty of scope now for adding decorative or even functional extras. Consider enclosing the spaces beneath the armrests, or even above them, to give better shelter from the wind. If you decide to add sides to the throne, consider a small roof, too, to recall the seats used in a medieval scriptorium.

Before you add too much extra, make sure that you give the tree house, especially the board, a good protective coat of exterior-quality varnish or fence paint. Think about using the paint to add to your decorative scheme. For inspiration, take a look at some classic thrones—real Gothic or Baroque thrones or mythical thrones, such as that of King Arthur or the Ice Queen.

At the points where the wooden pieces meet, you can add additional blocks or decorative cutout shapes to give the throne more bulk. You could add more pieces of 2 x 4s or thicker wood to all parts of the throne to make it more monumental.

You may want to use a chisel, gouge, or small ax to shape the wood slightly, combining this with scrolls or curves cut from plywood to give the throne more flowing lines. Lions' claws, eagles, serpents, unicorns, dragons, and an entire coat of arms can be added by cutting them from board with a saber saw.

You can also upholster the seat and the back, using a water-repelling foam and synthetic fabric. Camping mats make an ideal soft but nonabsorbent foam that can be held under vinyl sheets stapled into place. The Throne, nestled in its tree, should be a self-contained world. It would be good if it had a rope lift so that supplies can be hoisted up. A simple stepping-stone path to the foot of the ladder is also a nice touch.

90

SPOOKY HIDEOUT

Tree-house superstructures do not have to remain the same year in, year out, and some of the best ones are those added to over time. Hold an annual tree-house party as an excuse for exchanging one set of inventive walls for another If you're feeling theatrical, go to town on the themed approach. This tree house will make a Halloween night to remember,

and will continue to entertain until replaced by another. The Spooky Hideout relies mainly on inventive shapes used for the walls to give it character, making future conversions straightforward. Underneath the shapes that give it its distinct atmosphere lies a simple, walled structure and platform that use basic techniques for their construction.

PREPARATION

Prepare by cutting all wood in advance. This structure is built on the forked-tree platform described at the beginning of this section. Make sure that you have added any filling boards to cover exposed beams, depending on the nature of your tree. In the example here, we will assume a platform that is 4 feet deep and 8 feet long. If your tree-house platform is longer than this, simply construct the walls with additional lengths of board, using extra cutouts as needed to overlap the joints and to provide a method for attaching them together. If your tree-house platform is shorter, use smaller walls and decide which parts of the provided cutting pattern to omit.

Take a board for each wall and transfer the cutting diagrams to them. Feel free to adjust the profile design on the plans to suit your taste (test alternatives with paper cutouts) and remember that it will be easier to cut out the profiles on the ground before attaching them to the tree house. Follow the cut lines using a saber saw. The saber saw leaves a crisper cut on the underside, so the plans are drawn on the back face of the wood. The finished walls are, therefore, mirror images of the plans.

MATERIALS NEEDED FOR
SPOOKY HIDEOUT

In addition to materials listed for the Basic Platform *(see page 82)*, you will also require:

3 wall boards: ¾ inch x 4 x 8 feet
4 side wall side strips: 2 x 2 inches x wall height
2 side wall base strips: 2 x 2 inches x wall width
2 door posts: 2 x 2 inches x wall height
Doorway strengtheners: use triangular scraps from walls

FASTENERS
Screws: 2–2¾ inches, assorted

(CUTTING PLAN: PAGE 152)

AT THE TREE

First of all, construct a ladder for the tree house. Do this in a similar way to the ladder for the Throne, or any other project ladder in this book. You might want to add to the general air of spookiness by using uneven rungs with wood strips of varying shapes and sizes; if so, consider safety and ensure that the rungs are strong, well fastened, and not too unpredictable.

Lift the precut walls for the front and rear of the structure up to the side of the platform and secure them to the supporting branch-span beams. Make sure the walls hang down below the beams and use screws to fasten them to both top and bottom of the beam's face. If you are working alone, temporarily attach blocks to the platform side of each wall so that it can be lowered into position to rest on the blocks. The structure will be weak until you add your side walls, so be careful not to lean on it.

The side walls each need a length of 2 x 2 screwed flush to the bottom and side edges before they can be fitted. You will need to trim off the protruding ends. Once done, lift the walls into place so that they are sitting on the platform. Use the strips to screw them into place, flush with the platform edge and the other walls. Try using a single screw at the bottom of each touching wall first, then move to the top and align the wall edges before putting in a second. Once you have a good fit, add enough extra screws to make the joints very strong. Screw the base strips firmly down onto the platform.

If the doorway that you have used cuts its wall into two separate pieces, you will need to strengthen the entrance. This part of the tree house will get a lot of wear, so it needs some extra attention. Cut a 2 x 2 for each side to act as door posts and screw through the wall to hold them in place so that they rest firmly on the platform. You should then strengthen them either by adding a steel bracket or by fastening a triangle of wood to each of the door posts and then securing the triangles to the platform with short lengths of wood strips.

1. *Cutting out the wall profiles with a saber saw.*

2. *Adding the first side wall.*

3. *Adding the final side wall.*

4. *Strengthening the entrance with posts.*

WOOD STRIPS AND TRIANGLES

Adding diagonals strengthens a structure. If a square frame feels flexible, put diagonal strips across the opposite corners the frame to make it rigid. Any panel can be made more rigid by bracing it to another panel or the platform base by using a triangle of board attached with two wood strips. The principle of triangulation also works by paneling a whole frame with board, which is the same as adding a lot of diagonals.

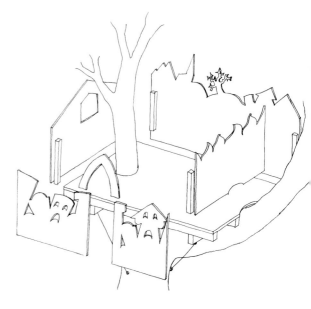

left *Build room dividers across the platform for extra fun. If you keep the front wall low, additional divider silhouettes will create a theatrical appearance. These are nonstructural, so aged or gnarled wood can be used—this, along with bent roofs and tilted walls, will add to the creepy feeling.*

right *An exploded view of the Spooky Hideout.*

FINISHING OFF

Check the points where the walls meet to make sure that the profiles look right next to each other. If not, trim some extra wood from the profile to make the corners work visually. Ideally, seeing both the different profiles at the front and the rear of the tree house overlaid should make the structure look fairly complex and interesting—like scenic flats on a stage. If you want to add compartments to the interior, make additional walls and secure them internally, using the same technique you used for the outer walls. In this way, it is possible to add an "inner sanctum" to the tree house or, by adding two dividers that cross each other, even a secret space. Dividers also provide a good fastening point for adding small, roofed sections.

PAINTING AND DECORATING

When it comes to painting the tree house, grays and muted browns are good for increasing the spooky atmosphere. Try to make any internal corners or spaces dark to lend a sense of mystery. Letting the darker paint run from corners over lighter painted surfaces will give the whole structure an organic, deserted look. You can drill some small holes and dribble a different shade of paint down from them so that the walls appear to be leaking. As with all tree houses, make sure that the structural elements, such as beams and boards, are all well sealed, but once that is done you can go to town on the finish. Overpainting again and again will add to its presence. Try using straw or sawdust thrown onto wet paint to give it a texture.

FINAL DETAILS

Once finished, a variety of additions will create the ideal Halloween haunt. Try, for example, broomsticks and black cats— either real or cutout in profile—and pumpkins placed around the base of the tree or lighting the path to the ladder. You can even summon your own resident ghost by draping a white cloth over a ball or balloon on the end of some string, hanging it from a higher branch so that it sways in the breeze. Encourage ivy or a similar creeper to trail itself over the structure. You can also make good use of any little monsters that you have hanging around.

Working with a Third Branch

Here are two possible variations on the forked-tree platform,
so that you can adapt this type of structure to accommodate
any peculiarities that your tree may challenge you with.
The following tree houses demonstrate the use of two
separate techniques. The first shows how to take
advantage of the rambling crown in a tree by
adding extra levels. The second deals with
creating a platform across more than two
branches and allows for a more ad hoc approach.
Always let the nature of the tree guide your choices.

PLATFORMS SPANNING THREE BRANCHES

Once you have established a platform across two branches as in the previous section, it is a relatively simple task to attach another platform above it, using the main platform to provide strength. In theory, you can add as many platforms as the tree offers fastening points, provided that your main platform is sturdy enough to take the extra weight.

The final project in this section elaborates on the technique that we have used previously for a forked tree to make it span three branches. There are many different ways of doing this, but for each of these ways the primary consideration other than strength is to build in an allowance for the separate branches to move independently of each other, especially if the tree is large.

A RECTANGULAR VARIATION

To adapt the previous platform for three branches, dispense with the support beam at one end and attach the other end of each branch-span beam directly to a separate branch. On the third branch, position a support beam in the same way as before; the branch-span beams can slide and twist while resting on it, with restraining blocks preventing them from sliding off. Because these branch-span beams are now mobile in relation to each other, it will be necessary to construct a solid platform with beams that rests across the branch-span beams and allows for slide. This platform is screwed down to only one of the branch-span beams. Where it sits on the others, it should be restrained with blocks that allow for a small amount of movement.

A TRIANGULAR VARIATION

A much more elegant option is to have a beam for each branch that spans beyond the next branch, making a triangle. Every one of these beams is then bolted to the branch at one end so that its other end rests freely on top of its neighboring beam near to where that one is bolted. As usual, the resting sections of beam are made captive within blocks so that they are able to slide.

This approach is very efficient and it minimizes the amount of wood needed for a strong, secure platform. Because each beam is both supported and resting, none of them are level. This demands a more intuitive approach to laying and leveling the platform. Luckily, such an intuitive approach is one of the best ways to build in such an organic form as a tree, and the triangular nature of this platform makes any square-base approach seem complicated.

The result is much more likely to be a tree house that appears to be a natural addition to the tree. The final project in this section uses this approach, taking the fantasy of a bird's nest big enough for a human cuckoo to inhabit, to emphasize this "responsive" way of working.

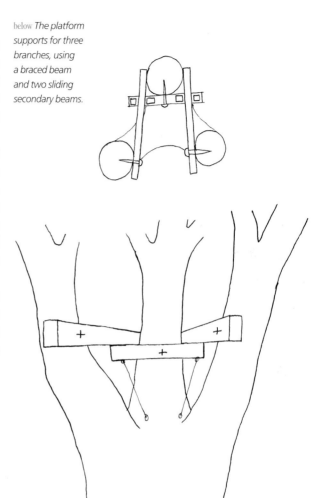

below *The platform supports for three branches, using a braced beam and two sliding secondary beams.*

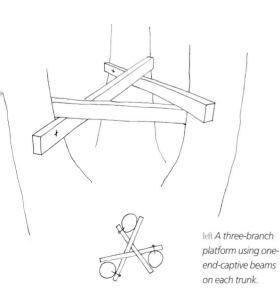

left *A three-branch platform using one-end-captive beams on each trunk.*

ADAPTATIONS

When planning an adaptation for your tree house, let the tree give you possible ideas. Look for places that beg to be included and imagine how they can be used. Remember that a small separate platform, such as a crow's nest, will add to the play potential of the structure and that there is nothing to stop you from including sloped platforms.

ENCHANTED CASTLE

This project develops the simple box theme that the Spooky Hideout was based on, with the same 4 x 8-foot platform. Again, the tree house uses theatrical cutout profiles, but this time to suggest fairytale castle shapes. An addition of a small upper platform makes the tree house look much more involved than its predecessor and some complex modeling

with flexible wood produce a substantial appearance There are many variations, so read through the instruction. and use them as guidelines fo your project. If you intend to add a number of platforms make sure that any fastening. are as strong as possible. Use larger bolts, increase the thickness of any wire rope, and use more substantial eyebolts.

MATERIALS NEEDED FOR ENCHANTED CASTLE

In addition to materials listed for the Basic Platform *(see page 82)*, you will also require:

FOR THE WALLS
5 boards: ¾ inch x 4 x 8-foot board
4 side wall side strips: 2 x 2 inches x wall height
2 side wall base strips: 2 x 2 inches x wall width
2 door posts : 2 x 2 inches x wall height
Doorway strengtheners: use triangular scraps from the walls
6 turret support strips (2 for each turret): 1 x 2 x turret height
3 plywood panel faces: ⅛ inch x 60 inches x turret height

FOR THE ADDITIONAL PLATFORM
1 support beam: 2 x 2 inches x platform width
4 upright supports: 2 x 4 inches x layer height
4 crossbeams: 2 x 4 inches x platform length
4 triangular supports: ¾-inch board
1 brace board: ¾ inch x platform width x layer height
1 platform board: ¾ inch x 4 x 4 feet
2 lengths of stainless steel wire rope of the correct thickness
4 wire rope thimbles
6 quick links or shackles
12 wire rope clamps
4 eyebolts with nuts and washers
2 screw eyes

PREPARATION

Prepare by cutting all the wood in advance. The Enchanted Castle is made up from a series of flat wall sections that must b cut from boards in the same way as the previous project, using the supplied cutting plan or designing your own. These wall vary from those of the Spooky Hideout in the way that they are assembled. Here, each wall will have a slot in it that slips into

FASTENERS
1 bolt: ½–¾-diameter, 8 inches long, with washer and spring washer
Screws: 2–2¾ inches, assorted

MATERIAL FOR ADDITIONAL PLATFORM WALLS
e.g. 6 curved supports: 24-inch radius, ¾-inch board
6 wood strips: 1 x 2 x 30 inches
3 plywood panel faces: ⅛ x 38 x 48 inches

(CUTTING PLAN: PAGE 154)

JOINING WALLS WITH SLOT AND WOOD STRIP AND OTHER TECHNIQUES

Two boards that cross each other at right angles can be easily attached by cutting a slot the thickness of a board halfway across each board at the point where they cross. Make sure that the slots are cut to accommodate the unslotted portion of the other board.

If your walls are too long for a single board, you can join them end to end by using a third short length of board to overlap the joint. Alternatively, run a wood strip across the two boards at the top and the bottom, then use one upright to cover the joint.

Often, the joining of boards can be avoided entirely by creative adaptation—how about a back door, a window, or even a slightly projecting balcony?

left The method of joining walls, showing slots and wood strip.

corresponding slot in its neighboring wall, much like children's cardboard toys. The slots need accurate cutting to allow for a board thickness to slide into them. We will use the overhanging parts of the walls to form a round tower at three of the corners from flexible plywood. For the added platform, we will use a 4 x 4-foot square of board, supported on 2 x 4 beams.

Transfer the cutting plans and cut out the wood. Exactly where the upper platform sits will differ from tree to tree, so you might need to make some additional cuts to the main platform's walls once the upper platform is located.

USING DISTANT BRANCHES

When adding an addition to the main platform, keep in mind the movement of the tree. A second level that uses the same trunk and fastened near the main platform will probably not move much in relation to the main platform and can be linked directly. When a distant location or a separate branch is used, you must allow for separate movement in any joining structure. Think of these as separate platforms and link them using rope ladders, nets, or gangplanks.

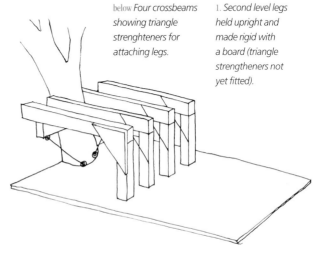

below Four crossbeams showing triangle strenghteners for attaching legs.

1. Second level legs held upright and made rigid with a board (triangle strengtheners not yet fitted).

1. Adding a slotted wall.

2. Adding the curved plywood to the turrets.

ADDING THE SMALL PLATFORM

First, identify the branch that will support the upper platform. It can be one of the branches used for the main platform or not, but it must be within 6½ feet of the existing platform edge and be strong enough to support a tree-house platform. Choose the height that you want the upper platform to be above the existing platform, and mark a fastening point for a bolt that faces the platform. Add a 48-inch-long support beam to the branch in the same way as for the existing platform, including the wire rope ties *(see page 81)*. Using a 1 x 2, rest it on the new support beam and hold it level over the center of the main platform to find the "layer height" from the main platform.

Make a support on top of the main platform to hold the other end of the upper platform's crossbeams. Do this by cutting four pieces of 2 x 4s to the layer height. Attach these to the end of four long crossbeams at right angles, using triangles of board to make four L-shaped components. The crossbeams must be long enough to overhang the support beam (to allow for slide) and to extend over the main platform's centerline (where its own central supports are). Evenly space the four long crossbeams on the new upper platform support beam so that the "legs" rest on the main platform. Hold them upright by screwing a brace board 4-foot wide and layer-height high across them all. As with the main platform, use blocks to trap the crossbeams so that they can slide on the support beam. Slip the new upper platform board onto the crossbeams and screw it down.

FITTING THE WALLS AND CORNER TURRETS

Identify which of the walls will be affected by the overhanging upper platform and cut away the areas where the walls and the platform intersect. Once you are sure that the walls will fit around the new upper platform, secure them to the supporting beams in the same way as for the Spooky Hideout, using side and base strips to secure the side walls. Strengthen the doorway.

In the other three corners, we will make corner turrets. Measure the length of the wall that protrudes from each corner. Mark a line down each wall at that distance from the corner and screw a 1 x 2 to the wall on the corner side of that line. Do this on both walls at each corner. Take a 38 x 48 inch-piece of ⅛-inch plywood board and nail it to the first wall strip. Slowly curve it around the wall ends. Finally, nail its far edge to the 1 x 2 on the wall around the corner. Repeat this for the two corner turrets.

Make sure that the walls are firmly attached to the upper platform where they are cut around it. If necessary, use wood strips to provide fastening points and fill gaps. To make the three curved walls for the upper platform, follow the instructions for the Platform Variation *(see page 64)*, then attach them to the upper platform, allowing space between the wall sections for the branch and also an entrance.

100

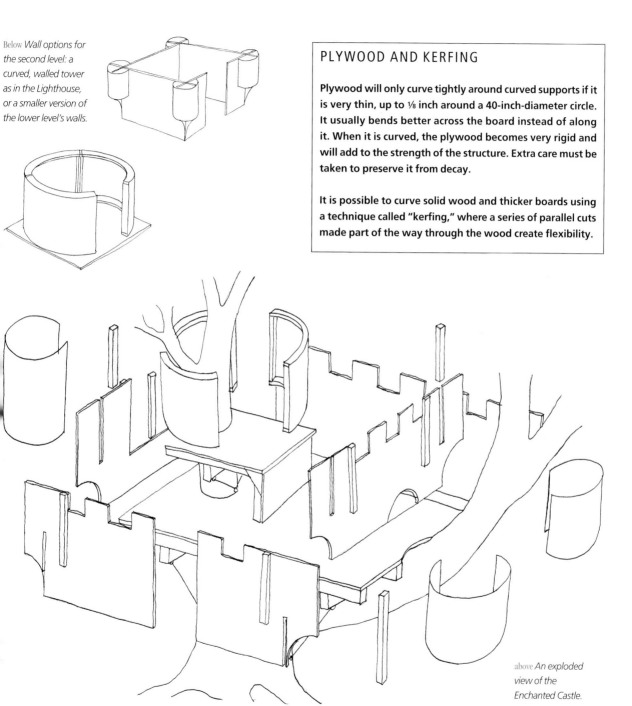

PLYWOOD AND KERFING

Plywood will only curve tightly around curved supports if it is very thin, up to ⅛ inch around a 40-inch-diameter circle. It usually bends better across the board instead of along it. When it is curved, the plywood becomes very rigid and will add to the strength of the structure. Extra care must be taken to preserve it from decay.

It is possible to curve solid wood and thicker boards using a technique called "kerfing," where a series of parallel cuts made part of the way through the wood create flexibility.

above An exploded view of the Enchanted Castle.

ENCHANTED CASTLE

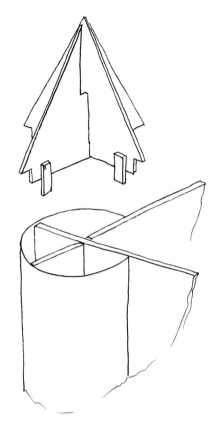

right *A method for making turret rooftops, showing how to attach the wood strips.*

around the tops of the turrets using thin plywood and spacers directly above the shaped walls so that there is something to fasten to. For access, choose one of the ladders described earlier.

PAINTING AND DECORATING

The Enchanted Castle should glow, so use cool colors to paint it, pale grays and even pale pinks and violets. You can add subtle silver highlights using aluminum spray paint, or perhaps hint at blocks of stone with faint gray shadows. If you are feeling brave, you can paint a billowing cloudscape on the lower walls. Paint the turret rooftops a variety of soft red shades. Whatever your chosen scheme, be careful to protect all structural wood and especially the boards from the effects of weather.

The project can be finished off with all the adornment you could possibly need in an Enchanted Castle: magic wands, a throne or two, and any glass slippers you happen to have at hand. Outside, you could consider an enchanted path leading up to it—spray some stones silver to guide the way. Rumor has it that golden apples and pears, frogs in ponds, and swords stuck in stones are all essential commodities for any desirable Enchanted Castle in the sky.

FINISHING OFF

Inspect the tree house for any parts of the walls that are not attached to the structure and screw them down, using wood strips or board spacers if necessary.

It is possible to make a pointed roof for each of the turrets by measuring across the turret and cutting two triangles with a base that is a little wider. Cut the same length slot in the top of one and the base of the other and slide them together. Place the point that results on top of the corner wall, over the turret, and attach it with wood strips and screws. Try to vary the height and angle of these rooftops.

Cut strips of castellated board and add to the outside of the wall tops. Screw them to the walls using wood strips as spacers to make them stand out a short distance. You can do the same

right *Some ideas for decoration details.*

BIRD'S NEST

For this tree house, we used a more intuitive approach than that of the other tree houses in the book. It represents a way of working that doesn't preplan every component. For many people, this is a more satisfying way to build because it allows you to be creative at every step of the process. For this type of platform support, we will cut some of the wood as it is needed, as the spaces to fill are unpredictable. This whole tree house could be made by just using sturdy branches, twigs, and brushwood. Even the board could be replaced with a party woven mat of straight saplings. Birds manage this tree house without the benefit of nails or screws; but, given the scale of our tree house, it is acceptable to assist nature.

MATERIALS NEEDED FOR
BIRD'S NEST

This list includes all the materials needed for the Bird's Nest, including the platform.

3 support beams: 2 x 4 inches x "branch-span" length
   plus 40 inches
1 platform board: internal diameter of the mean distance between
   the three forks
A variety of wood strips or logs and branches of different
   thicknesses
1 hoop: either cut from board or woven from saplings
6 posts to support the hoop: wall height
A large quantity of brushwood, trimmings, ferns, etc.

FOR THE LADDER
Wood for the ladder or blocks for making steps on the tree's trunk

FASTENINGS
3 bolts: ½–¾-inch diameter, 8 inches long, with washers
Screws: 2–2¾ inches, assorted
String
Wire

PREPARATION

Prepare by cutting wood in advance. This tree house is intended for construction in a tree with at least three branches. For extra branches, just add more main supports in the same way.

You will need one strong post, beam, or substantial branch for every branch that you will be attaching to. You will also need a good selection of reasonably straight wood or branches that vary from 2 inches thick to saplings ¼ inch thick. You will also need a quantity of dry brushwood or garden prunings.

For the platform deck, you will use a circle of board, but you can replace it by weaving a layer of strong saplings and adding crossing layers of mat, reeds, saplings, or planks until you are sure that there is no possibility of an arm or a leg poking through it.

One useful thing to prepare in advance is a hoop of wood, either by cutting one from board or by twisting a number of branches, willow, or bamboo poles into a large hoop and binding them with string. The hoop should fit easily between all of the branches that surround the location of the tree house and it will form the top of the inside wall of the structure.

THE SUPPORTING FRAME

To begin the supporting frame, be sure that you have support beams more than long enough to span between each supporting branch. Take the first support beam and place it level against two of the branches so that it extends beyond both of them. The end that will remain unfastened must be on the inside of the three branches, the fastened end on the outside. Use the familiar bolt technique to secure the outside end to the tree (the left-hand end in our example). Mark the level on the unfastened end's branch and then raise the loose end up until it is out of the way—tie it up, if necessary.

Now take the next support beam and do the same at the mark you have just made (so it is on your left hand, to continue the example). Move once more around the tree and do the same again, but this time before you attach the beam be sure it is sitting on the first beam that you attached (the overlapping beam will be on the right-hand side while you attach on the left). Once all three support beams are bolted at one end, carefully undo any that are tied up. The beams will all rest on each other.

SAPLING AND WITHY WEAVING

Saplings of hazel or willow are best for bending when they are freshly cut or have been soaked in water. Often, laying them out in the morning dew for a while will be enough. When you work them, try to twist them around each other as much as possible. That way, the natural spring of the wood will hold them together.

1. The free end of each beam is lifted with rope while the secured ends are bolted.

2. Weaving a hoop from saplings.

below The three beams placed to give the maximum supported distance; the trunks restrain the free ends.

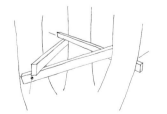

BIRD'S NEST

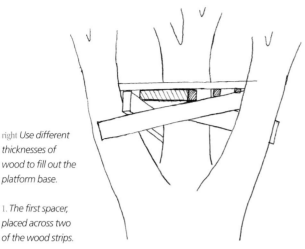

right *Use different thicknesses of wood to fill out the platform base.*

1. *The first spacer, placed across two of the wood strips.*

ADDING THE PLATFORM

This system has no beams that are level, so the next task is to establish a level platform that rests upon these main supports. You will do this by laying a circular board to fit between the three branches so that it finds a rough level by itself.

Then insert wood strips under the board to fill any gaps between it and the main supports. The first few of these spacers that we add are the most important—they are used to correct the level of the board and can be long enough to extend beyond both edges of the board, acting as spacers in two separate spots. The spacers will fit best if you don't try to make them parallel. Instead, find the direction that each spacer slips into most comfortably. As more are added, you may notice that previously fitted spacers get in the way and stop new ones from passing under the board; if so, keep them as long as possible. The beams will move in relation to each other, so any spacer must be long enough to support the board even if it slides.

If you are using branches and saplings instead of board, add plenty of them so that the thicker ends overhang the lowest point on a support and the thinner ends rest on the higher parts. Be sure to work from all sides of the platform as the spacers or branches must lay in every direction. Once you have a level platform, fasten the spacers down. For boards, screw downward into the spacers. For branches and saplings, use string or wire to bind them into a solid mat. Ensure that the platform will not be lifted off the supports in high winds by tying it to supporting beams in as many places as possible. If you need to strengthen the platform, add more fastenings and supporting spacers or branches.

BUILDING THE WALLS

Once you have a sturdy platform that will support the tree house and its occupants, take the hoop that you made and place it in the center of your platform. Cut at least six chunky posts to the same length—this length will determine the height of the Nest walls. Cut a hoop-size notch on the top of each one.

For a plywood base, set the posts upright in a circle so that the hoop is held in the notches. When the arrangement is stable, screw into the posts to fasten them. It will help to drill a series of holes through the board under the hoop to use for threading string through. Wind some string through these holes and up over the hoop to make it sturdy and make a lattice for binding the nest material to. For a branch base, attach the log posts one at a time using string to bind over the hoop and under the platform, pulling as tight as you can against the ends of the post.

Once you have a round fence with the hoop top securely attached to the platform, you can add the nest material. At first, bind bunches of rough prunings or wood thinnings to the outside. Build them up in layers, tying them in place, until the nest begins to resemble a chaotic, doughnut-shape bush.

2. *The leveled platform with the sapling hoop supported by the currently freestanding posts.*

Next, take long, supple individual saplings or withies from a willow tree and weave them into the bush and around the hoop to consolidate the walls. If you have used the plywood base, be sure to take enough of these woven elements and rough bunches under the edges of the board, fastening them with string or nails, so that the board is well hidden. Continue to add layers of woven sticks and bunches of bush until the walls of the nest are dense and sturdy. The chaotic mix of undergrowth, sticks, and string should knit together to form a resilient wall.

A LADDER OR THE NATURAL ROUTE UP?

If you are tempted to dispense with a ladder and use the trunk for a natural route up, consider how it might damage the bark of the tree first. It is better to attach good firm blocks or steps, using the same bolting techniques as for the platform. Never use a lot of small nails to fasten anything to the tree, and be very careful when climbing the tree.

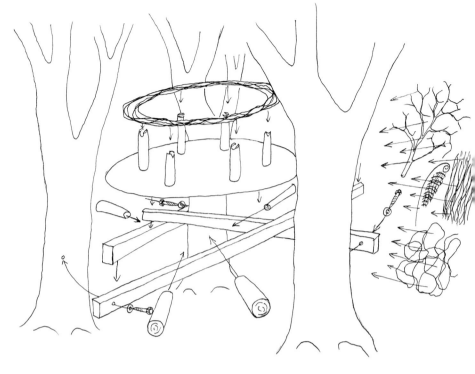

right An exploded diagram of the Bird's Nest tree house.

1. Weaving in brushwood, ferns, and prunings.

PAINTING AND DECORATING

As with all wood out in the open, you must protect it from the elements. In the case of this tree house, be sure that any sawn wood or board you used is well coated with a protective paint. Apart from that there is little scope for painting this structure. You can try making the construction even more solid by applying scrim or chicken wire and using mud, plaster, or a sticky, cement-base material, such as exterior tile adhesive to set the twigs and form a smooth central space. You may want to make the middle less twiggy by lining it with natural mats or even sewing synthetic carpet strips to the sides. Birds have a great advantage over us in having a free supply of down to line their nest. You will need to be inventive.

The Bird's Nest will look its best when it is as natural as possible. Ideally, it should merge with the surrounding foliage and only be obvious in silhouette or when you know it is there. You may wish to add a large egg-shaped backrest or two.

TREE HOUSES
FOR PAIRS OF TREE TRUNKS

INTRODUCTION

If you don't have a magnificent spreading tree, or even a large single tree, it is still possible to build a tree house by using several smaller trees and spanning your structure between them. This approach also gives scope for extensive tree house complexes that ramble among a wooded area of trees. In this section, we explore two ways of constructing platforms between trees. Although we keep the examples in this book at a low level for children, the principles can be adapted to make aerial walkways for adults. Combining these with the other techniques shown in this book, and by combining platforms, you can make multilevel structures that extend as far as you have trees to build in. If you have completed one of the other projects in this book, this section might give you ideas for adding to it in the future, and it will be an interesting challenge to make your addition fit with your existing tree house.

DIFFERENT POSSIBLE PLATFORMS

Building a tree house across two separate trees involves using similar strategies to those of the tree houses we built in the previous section. The main difference is that the distances we are likely to span are much greater, so the trees will move a lot more in relation to each other. Using this approach, you can base a functioning tree house on trees that would be too thin to support such a structure on their own. You must consider the strength of the trees that you intend to use and the size of your intended structure. If there is a large distance between the trees, the structure's weight will have more effect, so the trees will need to be more substantial. Because the trees are rooted separately, the wind will cause them to move independently. Allowance must be made for this movement, which will become more extreme the higher you build from the ground. In the case of

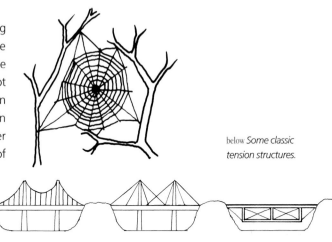

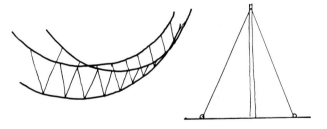

below *Some classic tension structures.*

MATERIALS NEEDED FOR
THE BASIC PLATFORM

Additional materials required for each project are listed on the relevant pages. For the Basic Platform, you will require:

Platform board: ¾ inch x 4 x 8-foot board
2 main support beams: 2 x 4 x 48 inches
4 secondary support beams: 2 x 4 inches x branch-span
   length plus 40 inches
6 spacers: about 2 x 4 x 14 inches
8 end-stop blocks: 2 x 4 inches
2 wood strips: 2 x 2 x length of base (8 feet), for the Car
2 wood strips: 2 x 2 x width minus 3 inches (45 inches), for the Car
2 wood strips: 1 x 2 x 48 inches, for the Car

FOR THE WIRE ROPE
4 lengths of stainless steel wire rope of the correct thickness
8 wire rope thimbles
12 quick links or shackles
24 wire rope clamps
4 bottle tensioners
4 eyebolts with nuts and washers
4 screw eyes

FASTENERS
Two bolts: ½–¾-inch diameter, 8 inches long, with washers
Screws: 2–2¾ inches, assorted

relatively thin trees, the wood that you attach to the tree may be strong enough to anchor the trees to each other, even at height.

For the four tree houses that follow, we will use two different types of platform. The first uses beams and braced fastenings, much like the tree houses in previous projects. This type of support is excellent for basing rigid types of tree house on or for making decks attached to single-tree-base structures.

The second type of platform is hung from secure fastenings so that the platform moves independently of the tree. This type of building takes its cue from tension structures, such as suspension bridges, but in our simplified form it has more in common with a hammock. This technique can be used at low levels for its ability to swing gently, or, when restrained with more fastenings, can form the basis for rope bridges and light platforms to connect separate tree houses high in the branches.

INTRODUCTION

113

The Basic Platform

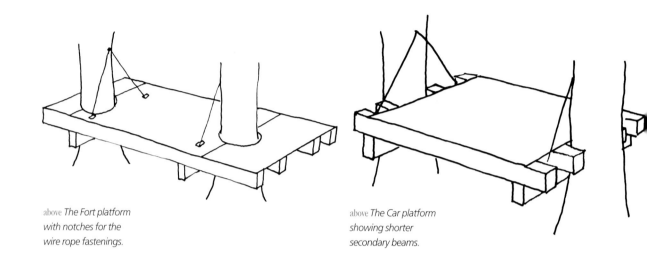

above *The Fort platform
with notches for the
wire rope fastenings.*

above *The Car platform
showing shorter
secondary beams.*

BASIC PLATFORMS FOR TWIN TREES

The next two projects use a platform supported on a beam fastened to each tree. These are braced to the tree to provide lateral stability in the same way as previous support beams in this book. Across these main support beams are arranged a series of smaller beams that slide upon the secured supports.

Both of these tree houses are built at a low level so that small children can enjoy them, so—unlike the previous projects—the support beams are braced upward because of lack of ground clearance. If you want to build higher, you have the choice of whether to brace downward or upward.

MEASUREMENTS FOR CHOOSING

When choosing a pair of trees for this project, keep in mind that we will be working to standard 4 x 8-foot board size. For the Fort, make sure that your trees are between 5 and 10 feet apart. For the Car tree house, there should be at least 5 feet of clear space between the trees. The trees should be at least 10 inches in thickness at your intended platform level.

PROBLEMS AND HOW TO DEAL WITH THEM

If the trees are slightly too close together or too far apart, you can still proceed, but you may need to cut some wood from the platform base or make it longer. If the trees have marked differences in thickness, the supports will need to be enlarged on the smaller tree to take account of the thickness of the larger one. Don't forget that you can add your own supports directly up from the ground. In fact, it should be possible to make these platforms with only one tree and several well-set posts.

It might be necessary to cut away brushwood or saplings that get in the way of your fastenings. Keep in mind that any branches growing toward the platform will interfere with it as they grow in the future. You can either prune incidental branches, or if they are substantial use them in your design.

SIZE DIFFERENCES

The next two projects differ in platform size. The size of the Fort will be dictated by the size of the trees and their distance apart. The platform will surround both trees entirely using cut boards to cover the support. The Car is made to a predetermined size and the supporting beams will be left exposed except where they support the body of the Car. The Car itself can be arranged diagonally to occupy the available space.

For these tree houses, we are using wire rope in tension to brace the main supports to minimize the clutter of using wooden triangular braces that we used for the first tree houses. If you prefer to use wooden braces, use them below the platform instead of above it as we have done.

It is possible to use any of the previous methods of fastening the main support beams, if you prefer. If this is the case, make sure that you allow for controlled movement in the secondary beams by using spacers and end stops. If your tree has old stumps or protruding dead wood from any past trimming, you can take advantage of these to fasten the supports.

SETTING FASTENING POINTS

Once you have decided upon the level of your platform, the first task is to mark a line around each tree that is at the same level. The best way to do this is to stand back and estimate the best position by eye to avoid any obstructions. Mark that height on one of the trees.

To transfer the level to the other tree, make a long-distance level. Take some clear hose or plastic tube long enough to reach the other tree with a sag in the middle. While holding both ends up in the air, fill the tube with water until the water can be seen just below both of the open ends. Ask an assistant to hold one of the ends of the tube up to the mark you have made on the tree while you walk to the other tree, being careful not to spill any water. Ask your assistant to tell you when the water level at their end is on the mark—you will need to move your end up or down to achieve this. When the water level is in line with the mark on the first tree, the water level at the other end of the tube

will give an exact level with that mark; mark the second tree. If you find the estimate was too high or low, use these established levels to mark lower or higher levels on both trees.

PREPARATION

Cut two main support beams to the length of 48 inches (standard board width), and drill a bolt-size hole in the center of the wider face of each of them. These main support beams must be at least 2 x 4s. Cut four secondary support beams so that when placed across the span between the trees they are long enough to extend 12 inches beyond both trees. The secondary support beams should also be made of 2 x 4s.

below *The important dimensions for a tree house with two trees:*
A = width between trees
B = overall width between the outer edges of the trees
C = width between centers of trunks
F = fixing height
P = platform height
W = width of trees

1. *Main support beams fastened inside the trees and braced with wire rope.*

below *Diagrams for fastening principles showing wire rope braced downward (left); wire rope braced upward (middle); and a triangle of board braced downward (right).*

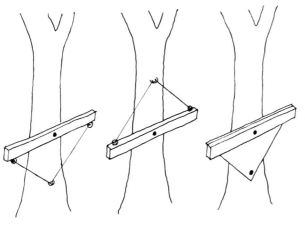

FASTENING THE MAIN SUPPORTS TO THE TREE

First, fasten the main supports using a single bolt through the hole that you have just drilled in each of them. The main support beams need to be fastened to the tree below the platform level mark that you have made. How far below depends on the thickness of the beams you are using. To find this distance, measure down from the mark on the tree the thickness of the platform, plus the thickness of the secondary beams, plus the distance from the hole in the main support beam to its edge. If you are using the wood in the cutting list, this distance will be about 6 inches. Make a pilot hole for the bolt this distance below the mark, so that the main support beams will be at right angles to the line between the trees.

Whether the main support beams are fastened between the trees or outside of the trees depends on which of the tree houses you are intending to build. For the Car, fasten them on the inside. For the Fort, fasten the main supports on either the inside or outside. If your trees are a long way apart and the secondary beams will have to span a long distance, it will be best to keep the main supports as close to each other as possible by fastening them on the insides of the two trees.

Once each of the main supports are bolted to the trees, they must be braced to prevent them from rotating. This can be done using wooden strips as in earlier projects or using stainless steel wire rope as described here.

On each tree, measure up 48 inches to a point directly above the bolt and screw in an screw eye. Drill a hole vertically right through the main beam, 3 inches in from each end, and insert a long eyebolt, so that the loop points upward. Be sure to use large washers on both ends of the bolt before you tighten the nut. Connect a length of stainless steel wire rope to each of the beam's eyebolts using wire rope clamps and thimbles. Make sure that there are three clamps at every joint and that the cable is straight and not caught on anything.

Cut the stainless steel wire rope to the length needed to reach the centered screw eye on the tree and attach them to two bottle tensioners hooked through the tree's screw eye

using three wire rope clamps per joint. Tighten the bottle tensioners in turn until the support beams are both level. (Find additional information on wire fastenings on page 81.)

BUILDING THE PLATFORM

The next stage is to add the secondary support beams and limit the amount that they can travel.

Rest the four secondary beams on their thin edges across the main support beams so that two are in line with the ends of the main beams and the inner ones are evenly spaced. Cut six 2 x 4 spacers to keep the secondary beams separated. Fill the three gaps above each main support beam with these and screw them down firmly. The secondary beams should be free to slide lengthwise and the two at the edge will even be free to move off the sides, at least for now.

Next, cut eight short blocks of 2 x 2s about 6 inches long and screw one of these to the underside of each of the secondary support beams, one at each end. These blocks must be fastened firmly to prevent the beams from sliding off the supports.

2. *Initial positioning of wire rope clamps on wire rope assembly.*

3. *The secondary beams restrained between the spacers on the main beams for the Car's basic platform.*

below *A cutaway view of the secondary beams showing restraining spacers on the main support beams.*

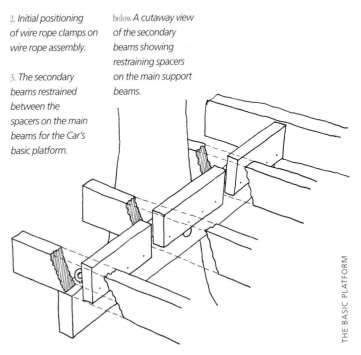

THE BASIC PLATFORM

117

1. *Adding the final end section of the platform board.*

2. *The completed platform that is used for the Fort. We placed the secondary supports inside the trunks due to the size of the trees.*

below *Exploded diagram of the Fort platform.*

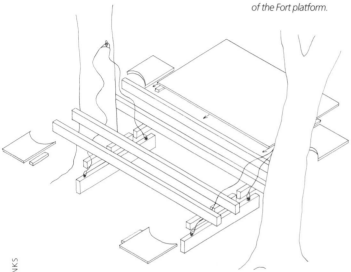

FOR THE FORT

Lay a sheet of board over the supports between the trees. Be sure that the edges are flush with the secondary support beams and screw through into each support beam using screws 12 inches apart. If there is plenty of space for the board, place it up to one trunk, with at least 1¼ inches of clearance, and add a short section of board to fill the gap up to the other one. If the space between the trunks is too short, remove a curve of board to clear the trunks. Mark the board by holding it in position, with at least 1¼ inches of clearance around the trunk.

Using the same technique, cut tree trunk profiles out of two more pieces of board and use them to cover the ends of the secondary support beams around the trunks. You will need to cut away four notches for the stainless steel tension cable.

If necessary, trim the last pieces of board with a handsaw so that the ends are square and they align with the ends of the secondary support beams. You may find it easier to use several smaller pieces of board to cover the platform; if so, make sure that the boards meet over the center of a support beam so that there is a firm fastening at each edge. Where the boards meet between the supports, add a wood strip beneath the joint so that you can screw firmly into it from both edges of the board. Make sure that there are no edges of the board that are not supported either with a beam or an added wood strip.

FOR THE CAR

Strengthen the platform board first. Cut two 2 x 2s to the length of 8 feet and cut another two to 45 inches long. Take a standard

4 x 8-foot sheet of board and screw the two longest strips along each of the long edges, so that the sides and ends are flush with the board. Next, screw the two shorter strips along the remaining edges of the board so that they fit within the strips that you fastened previously—again they should be flush with the edges. Finally, put two screws at the ends of the long strips through into the ends of the short strips. You should now have a board with a 2 x 2 frame around the edge.

Take this board and lay it either way up over the secondary supports. If you dislodge the two edge supports, simply replace them. This board will be the base for the Car, so arrange it so that it faces the direction that you want the Car to face while making sure that it sits across all the secondary support beams. You might like to sit it slightly diagonally to the supports—just make sure that it doesn't overhang more on one side than it does on the other. Once you have the platform base in the best position, screw down into the secondary support beams wherever possible. Make sure that you use plenty of screws and space them no more than 12 inches apart.

Take two lengths of wood strips the same length as the main support beams—48 inches if you are using the cutting list dimensions—and screw them across the secondary support beams directly above where they rest on the main support beams. These two strips will need to stop the secondary support beams from moving apart, so make sure that they are well fastened.

FINISHING OFF
Whichever tree house you are making, spend some time checking the structure for any loose or flexible parts. If you find any, strengthen them by adding wood strips or more board as necessary. Using a hand saw, cut off any ugly, protruding pieces of wood strip or board that you are sure do not need to be there for the strength of the structure. The stainless steel cable can, if you like, be made softer by covering it with a length of plastic pipe lagging or even a length of plastic pipe or hose. Finally, give the wire rope a final check and tighten it, if needed.

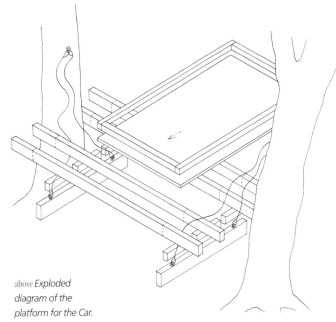

above *Exploded diagram of the platform for the Car.*

3. *Adding a wood strip to the Car platform.*

4. *The completed platform that is used for the Car.*

THE BASIC PLATFORM

FORT

Every den that a child makes is a space for the imagination; they become pioneers and adventurers and every detail can become the focus for a new fantasy. For this tree house, the fantasy takes place in a Fort. The theme takes its main cue from the Wild West, but it could just as easily be a scene from Treasure Island, Robinson Crusoe, *or even an ancient stronghold for a Roman army or a medieval stockade. Often, the most attractive tree houses are made from materials that are close at hand and have already become part of the scenery. We used natural logs for our project, but you can just as easily use the planks from an old picket fence, driftwood, or any other recyclable, worn wood.*

PREPARATION

Prepare by cutting all wood in advance. The majority of the wood needed for this structure is in the form of logs or planks that will be used for the walls of the tree house. The walls can be set at any height you like. If you have access to a supply of logs or a large quantity of rustic planks, you might like to make the walls very tall. For our version, we used precut logs for fences, which are available in most home-improvement centers. These come in standard sizes and are wired together in rolls.

The logs that you cut for the walls need not be cut to length too accurately—the Fort will look better if the tops of the walls are a little uneven. You can always vary the height of the wall to make crenellations in it and provide "cover" for the occupants. You can also space the logs on the walls apart slightly to make the wood go further.

WALL HEIGHT CONSIDERATIONS

When deciding upon the height for the walls of the Fort, keep in mind that the walls will cover the platform board and supports. This means that the walls will be about 8½ inches shorter on the inside of the tree house than they will appear on the outside. For safety, make sure that the height you have chosen is adequate to prevent the occupants from leaning too far out from the structure. Once you have decided how high to make the walls of your Fort, you need to make a frame onto which the log tops will be attached. This frame must be strong enough to support all the logs and act as a secure wall for the tree house. The frame is in the form of a rail that stretches from corner to corner at about two-thirds of the wall height. It is fastened to secure uprights at each corner and at two more for the gate.

1. *Fastening the wall uprights to the platform.*

2. *Fastening the top rail to the wall uprights.*

ESTIMATING WOOD AMOUNTS

The best way to estimate how much wood you will need is to think of it as an area of wood, in the same way that you would think of carpet or flooring.

Area is always referred to by measurements, such as "10 square feet." A good way to imagine this is to think of 10 tiles, each one being 1 foot long by 1 foot wide.

If you then imagine arranging these tiles you could make a row of single tiles 10 tiles long, or a rectangle 2 tiles wide and 5 tiles long. Both would be 10 tiles or 10 square feet in area.

To find the square area of the wood that you have, lay it out so that the logs lie next to each other like a raft and then measure how wide and how long the raft is. Multiply one measurement by the other, and your result is the square feet amount.

When you do this, make sure that the length of your logs will allow for the whole heights that you require to be cut from them without leaving scraps that are too short, as these will be wasted. Take these scraps into account and allow for more area than you need.

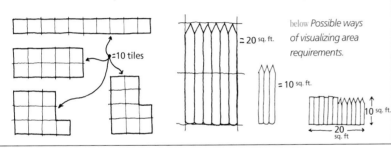

=10 tiles

= 20 sq. ft.

= 10 sq. ft.

10 sq. ft.

20 sq. ft

below *Possible ways of visualizing area requirements.*

FORT

To make the uprights for the wall frame, cut six 2 x 2s to length; they will need to be about two-thirds of the total wall height. The wall frame uprights should be firmly attached to the side of the secondary support beams at the corners of the longest edge of the platform. Use three 4-inch screws to attach each one of these uprights. Decide where you want the gate of the Fort to be, then attach a wall frame upright as a gate post on either side of the entrance. Again, the upright should be firmly fastened to the support beams using screws.

Cut five rails of 2 x 2s to span between the tops of all the frame uprights except the span across the gate. First attach the rail that spans right the way across the rear wall of the Fort, then the two shorter ones that span from the corners to the gate posts. These rails should be screwed down into the top of the wall-frame uprights.

Next, add the two side rails by fastening them on top of the front and rear rails that you have just attached, being careful to avoid the screws that are holding the previous

rails. To finish the wall frame, cut five lengths of 2 x 2s to fit between the bottom of the uprights. Screw these to the support beams, where they will act as spacers that will keep the log walls vertical.

THE GATE

Before you add the walls to the structure, it is a good idea to concentrate on the gate while you have clear access to any fastening points that you might need.

Take two substantial logs or posts that are long enough to make gate posts and that suit the type of doorway you want. If the doorway is to have a cross member or ranch sign, make sure that there is plenty of height so that the occupants will not bang their heads as they enter or leave the tree house now, or in the future. If you only want basic posts, make them slightly longer than the wall logs. You can fasten these posts to the wall frame uprights either externally or on the inside of the platform. They should be attached by screwing through the wall-frame

USING A COUNTERBORE

If the wood or log that you want to attach is too thick for a screw to pass through, you can always use a counterbore. A counterbore is similar to a countersink, where you drill a small shallow depression so that the head of the screw sits slightly below the surface of the wood. A counterbore is where you drill an extra-wide hole partially through the wood so that the screw's head can pass down deep into the wood before it begins to grip. To make a counterbore, use a pilot drill as usual, then select a drill bit that is wider than the screw's head and use this to widen the pilot hole for part of the thickness of the wood. Be careful not to be overenthusiastic with the counterbore drill, and make sure that you don't drill too deep and end up weakening the wood and leaving nothing for the screw to grip on.

1 *Adding a ranch sign using a rough piece of wood.*

2. *Using the rungs to fasten two scaffold boards together for the ladder.*

3. *Paneling the walls with poles.*

upright into the post using long screws. Be careful that no sharp screws emerge through the other side of the wood, because this could cause injury.

COMPLETING THE WALLS

Once the gate posts are attached, you can begin to add the rustic logs to the walls. Start at the gate and work around toward the rear of the Fort. Each log should be attached by first drilling a pilot hole in the wall rail and then screwing through from the inside of the tree house. Once the top screw is in, you should add another at the bottom, but this time from the outside of the wall into the wood strip that you applied to the secondary support beams.

If you are using thick logs, you may need to counterbore the pilot holes to enable you to get a good screw fastening. It is a good idea to do all the top screws first, then to go outside and finish all the bottom ones. Make sure that each log is well fastened and secure—if any are still movable, add another long nail through into the support beam.

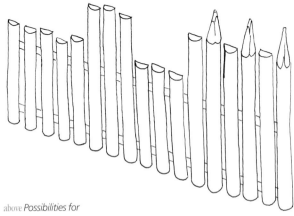

above *Possibilities for the top of the walls.*

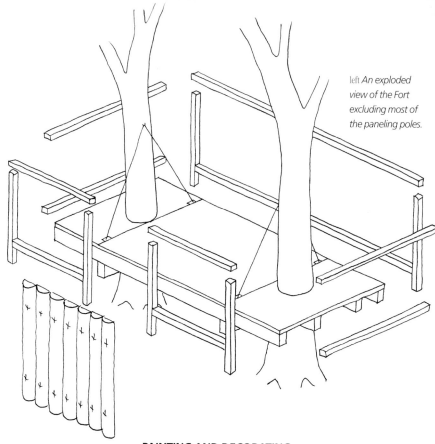

left *An exploded view of the Fort excluding most of the paneling poles.*

FINISHING OFF

Once you have filled all the walls' length with logs, you just need to add a ladder and a ranch sign over the doorway. You can use any of the ladder types mentioned in this book, but a style that suits the Fort well is a gangplank ladder. To make one of these, you will need one or more sturdy planks long enough to lean at a shallow angle up to the entrance way. Rest the planks in position and fasten them to the platform at the top, using screws, bolts, or brackets. Cut lengths of 1 x 2s to cross the boards horizontally and screw them to the boards so they are evenly spaced all the way to the top. They will serve as rungs and hold the boards together.

For the ranch sign, use a thin plank of wood that will span across both of the gate posts and screw it across the top of the entrance. The ranch sign will look best if you choose a piece of wood that has some character, perhaps some rough-sawn lumber with its bark still on it.

PAINTING AND DECORATING

The Fort will, as with all tree houses, need to be protected from the elements by using exterior fence paint or varnish on all board and sawn wood, especially the structural parts. You don't need to protect any natural logs if they are substantial enough, although it is wise to seal the tops with paint.

The ranch sign can be painted with the name of your Fort, or if you are feeling adventurous, try cutting out the letters with a saber saw, or adding shapes onto it, such as wire letters, horseshoes, or cow horns.

FINAL DETAILS

Once the structure is built, you can add a small shelter or lean-to inside the walls by adapting the techniques used throughout this book. On the ground, an arrangement of whitewashed rocks along the path to the ladder and around the perimeter will give a military impression good enough for the cavalry.

CAR

Tree houses transport everyone into a fantasy world, and this one doubles the effect by making a magical car that is suspended from the trees. Who hasn't at one time or another wished for a flying car? This tree house is open to a great deal of interpretation. The Car can be styled to resemble a familiar family car, or built to look like a classic.

Spend some time researching famous cars, both real and imagined, and make sketches. Ask the drivers what cars they like. Chitty Chitty Bang Bang and Harry Potter's car were vintage classics, as are pink Cadillacs. Movies are a great reference point—remember the space-age car in The Fifth Element *and the convertible in* Thelma and Louise?

MATERIALS NEEDED FOR CAR

In addition to materials listed for the Basic Platform *(see page 113),* you will also require:

1 board for: ⅜ inch x 4 x 8 feet bonnet panels and wheels
3 boards for sides, seats, bulkhead, front, rear, boot: ¾ inch x 4 x 8 feet
Car body strips: about 1 x 2 inches x 26 feet required
Windshield strips: 1 x 1 inch x 10 feet or enough for surround
1 board for facing front wings: ⅛-inch plywood

FASTENINGS
Screws: 2–2¾ inches, assorted
Small nails for fastening plywood facing

MISCELLANEOUS
4 tires (optional)

(CUTTING PLAN: PAGE 156)

PREPARATION

Appearances are deceptive. This is a simple structure based on a series of boxes. The "intricacy" is due to using a few cut profiles and some flexible plywood. The profiles that we have provided on the cutting plans can be customized if you have a specific car in mind. Just spend a few moments looking at how the sections fit together and you should be able to make the right changes. If you want to seriously alter the shape of the Car, we suggest that you cut out your profiles to scale in thin cardboard, and test your changes on a small-scale cardboard model.

Begin by cutting out the two side sections of the Car. Transfer the profile from the cutting plans to the wood and cut out the first one with a saber saw. Then use the first one as a template for the second one to ensure that they match. Next, cut out the front, the bulkhead, the seat back, the seat, and the rear. Make sure that you transfer all the dotted lines that show where to attach wood strips onto the panels. While you are set up to cut out profiles, finish cutting all the remaining ones you want to use, such as the wheels, bumpers, headlights, etc.

AT THE TREE

Decide which direction your Car will be facing and fasten the front panel to that edge of the platform by screwing it to the framing strip that is attached to it. Then take both of the side panels and fasten them to the appropriate sides of the platform in the same way. Cut two short 1 x 2s to join the front panel to the sides at the corners. Make sure that they are joined flush where they touch.

Next, you need the two 1 x 1s to act as the side edges of the windshield. Measure the required height from the floor of the platform to the top of the windshield and cut them both. Inside the Car, align these windshield side strips to the front edge of the door openings and screw them to the sides; make sure that they are both at the same angle when you view the Car from the side.

Get the bulkhead panel and slide it between the side panels into the engine space so that it rests against the two strips that you have just added. Fasten this down with screws. Measure the distance between the windshield sides at the top of the bulkhead. Cut a length of 1 x 2 to this dimension and fasten it between the tops of the windshield sides using two screws at each end, screwing through from the outside of the Car.

In a similar manner to the windshield strips, cut two more 1 x 2s to locate the seat-back profile and make them long

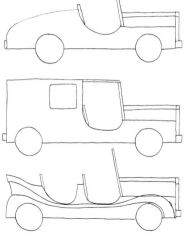

1. *Cutting out the side wall profile.*

2. *Adding a seat support strip.*

3. *Adding the windscreen side strip to the bulkhead panel.*

4. *Two panels fastened with a short strip.*

left *Possible variations for the side walls. These would be cut to the lowest hood line.*

enough to extend to the top of the side panel. Slide the seat-back panel into position in front of the new strips and fasten.

To support the seat panel, fasten two short lengths of 1 x 2s to the inside of the Car sides, ¾ inch below the door openings. Join them with a 1 x 2 that stretches across the front of the seat-back panel. Make sure that all these strips are firmly attached, then drop in the seat panel against its supports. Don't fasten it yet because you may need to remove it for access later. Add the second row of seats in the same way as the front seats.

CAR

below *The basic structural plan of the battens and panels.*

1. *Adding the curved plywood to complete the hood.*

2. *Positioning the trunk panel on its strips.*

3. *Positioning one of the hood panels.*

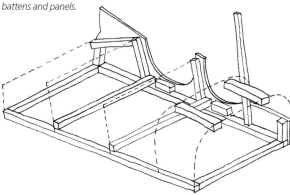

To construct the hood, fit the two 1 x 2s that span between the bulkhead and the front of the Car into the positions shown in the diagram on this page, then screw through the board to hold them. Take the 1/8-inch plywood cut to the dimensions shown on the plan and place it over the hood so that its centerline aligns with the centerline on the bulkhead. At this center point, nail the hood down to the bulkhead and the front panel. Working outward, wrap it over the hood, nailing as you work, until the last edge is flat on the side panel. If necessary, use more nails to make it hug the curve and lay flat on the sides.

Next, fasten the rear panel to the platform, making sure it is on the inside of the 2 x 2 edging the platform. Use two lengths of wood strips to connect it to the rear of the car sides. The exposed strips at the rear will hold the rear bumper. It may be necessary to cut a notch to clear the windshield post.

Screw a wood strip along the top edge of the rear panel, followed by another behind the seat—just below the top. Place the hood panel across both strips and fasten it with screws.

COMPLETING THE STRUCTURE

Place two pieces of 1 x 2s as spacers behind the radiator panel and screw the whole assembly to the center of the front panel. Use the strips supporting the trunk to attach the two hood flaps to, using loose screws so that they slope down and rest on the hood. Fasten the hood flaps to the front panel with screws or nails. At the bulkhead, you can provide extra support by attaching a small extra triangle of scrap board.

Cut four circles from board to make the wheels of the car. To attach the wheels, identify the points on the car where the wheels have the best visual impact. Then you should check for any obstructing beams. If there are any, it will be necessary to cut the wheel in two, so that part of it can be placed alongside the beam; then the remaining part can have a notch removed so that it can be fitted as well. Screw the wheels directly onto the car's side panels.

If you would like to have a trunk that opens, simply cut a hole out of the trunk panel and place a slightly larger "lid" over it. Use hinges to fasten the lid into position. Bumpers and lights can all be cut from board and fastened to the main panels, depending on the type of car you are making and how you want to customize it.

USING REAL TIRES FOR THE WHEELS

Instead of using wooden circles for the wheels you can substitute four real tires. To fit them around any obstructing beams, cut right through the tire using a hacksaw, then ease it over the problematic beam. It may be necessary to cut a small notch from the tire using metal shears. Consider relocating the wheels slightly to make fitting them easier—it won't matter if the wheels aren't exactly symmetrical on both sides of the car. Be careful when cutting the tires—clamp the tire firmly to a bench by its inside rim and always wear thick gloves when cutting them. To attach the tires to the side panels, use ordinary screws.

4. Cutting a tire
with a hacksaw.

5. The basic Car
structure complete.

PAINTING AND DECORATING

The possibilities for painting this tree house are endless. Whatever color scheme you have in mind, make sure that you don't overlook the classic "go-faster stripes," two-tone effects, racing car numbers, taxi checkers, and police car markings. It is a good idea to paint the interior a separate color and consider painting on all the interior details with a fine brush. Be sure to include a lot of switches and dials on the dashboard. Because the tree house is made mostly from board, it is essential that you paint it with a protective weatherproof paint even if you only use it as an undercoat for more inspired glossy finishes.

FINAL DETAILS

You can cut a circle from leftover board to make a steering wheel. Attach this by screwing a thick block of wood to the bulkhead in front of the driver's seat and attaching the wheel with a bolt through its center. The play value of the tree house is in the detail and there is no shortage of car equipment available. Consider adding an old rear-view mirror or buy a cheap stick-on one, and try hub caps, lights, hood mascots, and fluffy dice. The support beams that remain exposed can be boarded over and disguised as a road surface with some mineral felt, or given profiles that look like a landscape.

below *An exploded view of the Car structure.*

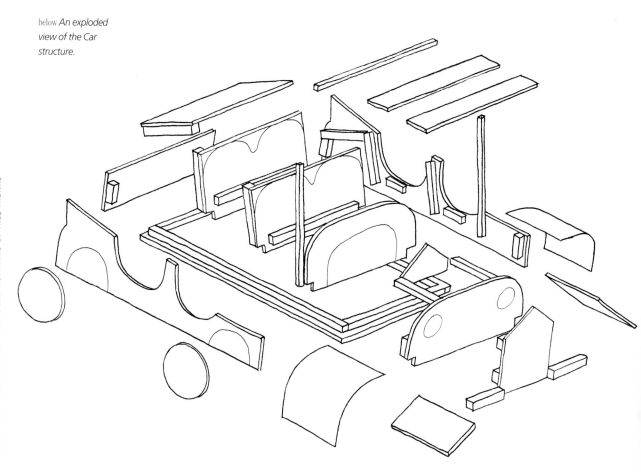

Swinging Platforms

Although it is possible to limit the movement of the platforms using extra cables, we will take advantage of this inherent mobility and imagine a tree house as a glorified swing. You will construct the platform so that it can be swung a limited amount, depending on the fastenings that are possible with your tree. These platforms obviously carry some inherent dangers—as heavy objects they will knock into anything in their way with a great deal of force. However, when used responsibly, they really are a whole lot of fun.

SWINGING TREE HOUSES

The remaining two tree houses in this section use a completely different method of attaching the platform to the tree. The platforms are suspended from eyebolts using stainless steel cable. This technique has a minimal impact upon the trees because the tree houses themselves are not in contact with their trunks. It also means that the tree houses are far more mobile than any of the other versions in this book and will not restrict the natural movement of the trees.

If you are considering making one of these tree houses, you must be aware that they will swing. Care must be taken to

make the vicinity as safe as you would for any swing. These tree houses should not be built too high up from the ground and the area beneath the platform should be kept clear. If you are concerned about the safety of having a swinging tree house, use a rope to restrain its movement.

The structure consists of two elements: a rigid platform and a supporting system of cables. The platform acts as a rigid base that will not bend and will provide solid fastening points for the supporting cable. As the platforms for the two tree houses are different, the detailed instructions for making them will be covered under the separate project instructions.

1. A screw eye fastened into the tree.

2. Eyebolts fastened through the substantial thickness of the beams.

3. The completed hanging platform.

low, the platform will be less stable but will not swing for long when pushed. If they are high, any swinging will last for quite some time but it will be a more gentle motion. The choice of height is a compromise between these two choices; aim to get the fastenings at least higher than the platform is wide.

Each platform has four fastening locations where an eyebolt is attached to solid supporting beams. When drilling the holes for the eyebolts, you must ensure that they pass through the center of the main beam and that the wood is in good condition. The eyebolts must be used with washers and lock nuts.

HANGING THE PLATFORM

Hang the basic platform before adding any extra structure to it. First, attach a cable to each tree screw eye by looping it through the screw eye over a thimble. Use three wire rope clamps to clamp the returning end of cable back to itself, making sure that the thimble is tightly gripped in the loop of the cable. Raise the platform up on temporary supports to the height that you require. Fasten a bottle tensioner over each platform eyebolt, making sure that it is half open. Then join the cable to the bottle tensioner in the same way as you did to the tree screw eyes, making sure that each cable is as tight as possible without any snags. Once the cables are all connected and the fastenings are sound, remove the temporary supports. (See page 81.)

The cable system comprises tree and platform fastenings linked with stainless steel cable that is under tension when the structure is complete. The tree fastenings are four screw eyes, two for each tree, one on either side of each trunk. Using two fastening points on each tree helps to limit the amount that the platform will swing. The platform fastenings are bolted through the main supports of the platform. There are four of these, one at the front and one at the rear of each side of the platform.

The fastenings on the tree must be well above the platform level. The height that you choose for them will have an effect on the way that the swing behaves. If the fastenings are too

MAGIC CARPET

The Magic Carpet is a simple tree house to build and can be used as the basis for many other swinging tree structures, such as swing seats. It could even be used as an alfresco table. To create the effect of a carpet flying on the wind, we've undulated the surface to give a ripple effect. This is done using curved supports running along the support beams

covered with a thin plywood facing. Curved plywood is unexpectedly strong, and as long as the surface is not pierced with sharp objects (no stilettos), it will support a substantial load. Remember that this structure will swing and consider safety as you plan its dimensions. Then hop on, summon your genie, and enjoy the wind in your hair.

MATERIALS NEEDED FOR
MAGIC CARPET

This list includes all the materials needed for the Magic Carpet, including the platform.

FOR THE BASIC CARPET
1 platform board: ¾ inch x 4 x 8 feet
2 long platform support beams: 2 x 4 inches x 8 feet
5 short platform support beams: 2 x 4 inches x 45 inches

FOR THE WIRE ROPE
4 lengths of stainless steel wire rope of the correct thickness
8 wire rope thimbles
12 quick links or shackles
24 wire rope clamps
4 bottle tensioners
4 eyebolts, with nuts and washers
4 screw eyes

FASTENINGS
Screws: 2–6 inches, assorted
Small nails for fastening plywood facing

FOR THE FRINGED CARPET
1 board for fringe and curved supports: ¾ inch x 4 x 8 feet
1 board for curved facing: ⅛ inch x 4 x 8 feet

(CUTTING PLANS: PAGE 151)

The platform that is required for the Magic Carpet is a simple rectangular shape based on a single 4 x 8-foot board. Cut it to 46½ inches x 8 feet if making the undulating version. Cut two pieces of 2 x 4s to the same length as the board (8 feet) and fasten these flush with the longest edges of the board using plenty of 2½-inch screws.

Cut five pieces of the same 2 x 4s so that they fit tightly between the two beams that you have just secured. Place two pieces flush with the remaining short ends of the board and space the other three evenly between them. Fasten them all firmly with plenty of screws through the board. Now fasten the beams themselves together by screwing through the long beams into the ends of the shorter crossbeam. Use 6-inch-long screws for this purpose. You should now have a sturdy, solid platform that is almost ready to suspend.

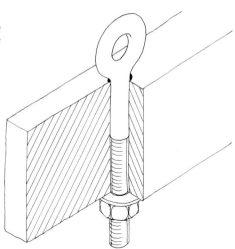

1. *The simple hanging platform is supported while the wire ropes are fastened.*

right *A cutaway view of an eye bolt fastened through a drilled beam. Note the washer.*

Before it can be suspended, an eyebolt must be added at each corner to which to attach the stainless steel cable. Attach each of the eyebolts by drilling a hole right through the board and the center of the long beam. The hole must be no nearer than 4 inches to the end of the beam.

AT THE TREE

Once you have attached the cables to the tree eyebolts as we described at the beginning of this section (*see page 133*), take your platform and put it between both trees.

Position the platform where you want it to be so that its center is directly between the two trees. Support the platform in this position a little above the height you want it to occupy. Add a bottle connector to each platform eyebolt and connect the cable from the nearest tree eyebolt to each one. Try to make the cable as tight as possible between the two eyebolts. It is important that you use four separate cables with a good connection at each end; do not attempt to save effort by using a loop of cable through any two of the fastenings.

ESTIMATING THE REQUIRED CABLE THICKNESS

Wire rope comes in many varieties and should be matched to the load it will support—ask your supplier for details. For safety, you should never exceed 20 percent of the rope's strength.

To calculate the thickness of rope that you need, add the following factors from your tree house:

For each board: 110 pounds
For each 33 feet of 2 x 4s: 110 pounds
For each 65 feet of 2 x 2s: 110 pounds
For each 130 feet of 1 x 2s: 110 pounds
For each occupant: 175 pounds (330 pounds for larger adults)

When you have accounted for every item that will add weight to the structure, multiply the total by five and you will have the minimum breaking load for the cable that you will require. You should then use the diameter of wire rope with a higher breaking strength.

SAFETY ALERT!

Consider the height of the platform carefully. Try to avoid the possibility of anybody getting themselves trapped by the platform as it swings. It is better to have at least 1¼ inches of ground clearance than to make it too low, but for it not to be so high that it could bang somebody's head.

1. *The Magic Carpet as a plain, flat structure.*

2. *Adding plywood over curved supports to make an undulating surface.*

FINISHING OFF

To complete the effect of the carpet flying, you might like to add a fringe that will give the carpet a flowing appearance. To do this, cut out the end covers and the straight side formers (C2) shown on the cutting plan (*see page 151*). Cut them from plywood and screw them on to the sides of the support beams so that the tops are flush with the platform's upper surface.

If you want to give the Magic Carpet an undulating surface, cut out the extra curves, or fins, shown on the cutting plan and use the side panels with the undulating tops (C1). Fasten the sides so that the top corners are in line with the platform's upper surface. Then evenly space the extra curves across the top surface of the platform so that the same bumps are next to each other. Fasten using scraps of 1 x 2s. Face the whole surface with ⅛-inch plywood, using nails to fasten it to the tops of the profiles. The more fins you use, the stronger the surface will be.

If you choose to leave the platform flat, you can always make the undulating carpet effect whenever you need it by draping cloth or a real carpet over the platform and making bumps by using blankets, foam, or bundles of cloth. That way the tree house need never be wet when it is used.

PAINTING AND DECORATING

It is important that the tree house platform is painted in order to preserve it, including the underside. Use an exterior-quality wood preservative paint to protect all the exposed wood. The carpet itself will look much more exotic if it has an intricate pattern. Try using a template to mark out repetitive shapes in pencil, then fill them in and elaborate on them using paint. A band of tassels painted around the base of the fringe that is leaning with the wind will produce a moving effect. The cables can be disguised with swags of cord.

FINAL DETAILS

Silks, tassels, velvets, and jewels will all help set the scene for a journey on the Magic Carpet. Scatter cushions over the platform and keep your sandwiches in straw baskets. An exotic-looking bottle could be full of lemonade or perhaps contain a genie? It is said that the pilot should always wear a turban and that an old oil lamp could be useful in emergencies.

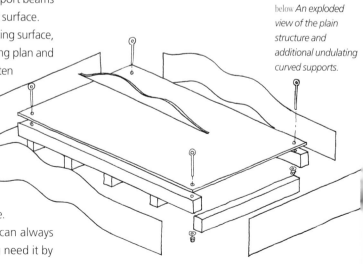

below *An exploded view of the plain structure and additional undulating curved supports.*

PLANE

Everyone can benefit from getting away from it all and what better way is there than having your own plane? This one will move just enough to give a real sense of flying but be firmly anchored just above the ground. It is not difficult to build and it can be easily adapted to become a jet. The structure itself uses the ability of most plywood boards to bend

slightly, creating a graceful fuselage that is supported by strong beams and stainless steel cable. Finishing the Plane with aluminum paint will give it a spectacular silver finish. Alternatively, there is always the Red Baron look. For younger pilots, buy a storybook featuring a plane, then match the design and watch their imagination take off.

MATERIALS NEEDED FOR PLANE

This list includes all materials for the Plane, including the platform.

4 fuselage and wing support beams: 2 x 4 inches x 8 feet
1 wing platform board: ¾ inch x 4 x 8 feet
1 board for base, tail, propeller, etc.: ¾ inch x 4 x 8 feet
1 board for both side panels: ⅜ inch x 4 x 8 feet
1 board for fuselage top panels: ⅜ inch x 4 x 8 feet
8 named wood strips (A, B, C, D): 2 x 2 x 24 inches
2 nose fastening wood strips: 2 x 2 x 24 inches

FOR THE WIRE ROPE

4 lengths of stainless steel wire rope of correct thickness
8 wire rope thimbles
12 quick links or shackles
24 wire rope clamps
4 bottle tensioners
4 eyebolts, with nuts and washers
4 screw eyes

FASTENINGS

Screws: 2–2¾ inches, assorted
4 carriage bolts: 6 inches

(CUTTING PLAN: PAGE 158)

ASSEMBLING THE PLANE ON THE GROUND

The platform that is required for the Plane consists of a cross of beams strengthened with board. Cut four beams from pieces of 2 x 4s to the length of 8 feet and cut a 3 x 8-foot panel from a standard board. Screw one beam flush with the edge of the panel and fasten the second one parallel to it on the same side of the board 24 inches away. This long platform will be the wing assembly and the edge with the flush beam is the front. Mark a line across the wing at its middle point and measure 12 inches either side of that line at the front.

For the fuselage assembly, place the two remaining beams so that two ends are touching and the other two ends are 24 inches apart. Cut a rectangular board 12 x 24 inches and

1. *The wing assembly ready for adding the fuselage assembly.*

2. *The fuselage assembly added to the wing.*

3. *Bolts fastened through both fuselage beams, one facing in each direction.*

place it over the separated ends of the beams so that its long edge is exactly in line with the ends. Screw the rectangular board down to both beams, being careful to keep them at the same angle to each other. Screw a small strip of plywood across the bottom of the two beams where they touch to join them.

Place the wing assembly on some blocks to raise it up from the ground—make sure the board is on top. Place the fuselage assembly across the center of the wing assembly, using more blocks to support it. The rectangular board must be on the bottom of the two beams. Arrange the fuselage assembly so that the rectangular board is placed neatly up against the wing assembly and the two beams are in line with the two 12-inch marks that you put on the wings earlier. To fasten the two assemblies together, drill a hole for a bolt through both beams at each of the four points where the beams cross. Insert a long carriage bolt through each hole as you drill it to make sure that the holes all align, then once you have inserted all four bolts, add washers and tighten completely. Turn the whole platform over and screw through the wing board into the fuselage beams.

Identify the four cable anchoring points. There is one at the front end of each wing and one on either side of the rear of the fuselage, where the support beams meet. Attach the eyebolts for the cable. On the wings, drill a hole right through the board and the center of the beam 4 inches from its end. At the end of the fuselage, drill two holes right the way through the center of both beams, and add an eyebolt to each hole.

PLANE

1. *The Plane platform suspended.*

2. *The nose panel fastened to the platform beams, showing strips A and B.*

3. *Fastening the side panel while bending it to the base curve.*

AT THE TREE

Before continuing, suspend the platform from the tree fastenings *(see page 81)*. Once you have done that, cut out the profiles for the Plane's body that are shown in the cutting plan *(see page 158)*.

Take the body base panel and rest it on top of the fuselage beams. Make sure that it is centered and that its front is flush with the two beams at the front. Screw it down to the beams using plenty of screws.

Take the nose panel and screw it to the front ends of the beams so that its bottom edge hides them. Make sure that it is upright and level. Measure back from the nose panel 12 inches and make a mark on the floor of the body base, calling it A. Make another mark called B, 40 inches back from A. Make one called C, 12 inches farther back again from B. Then, finally, mark D, 12 inches back from that. At each of these marks measure the width of the body base and cut two wood strips to that length. Name each one after the mark it corresponds to and write it on them. Take each one of these strips and screw them across the base directly at their mark.

Take one side panel and rest it in position on the wing so that the front is touching the nose panel. Screw it to the nose panel using a short wood strip on the inside of the corner, then bend the panel toward the body base, adding a screw into the end of each of the named strips as you work, until you reach the end of the side panel, where you can screw into the beam.

4. Fitting the tail into the slot in the upper body panel.

5. Positioning the upper body panel before bending it over the supporting strips.

and down into the strip. Take the rear top panel and rest it across the B, C, and D strips, like you have just done with the front top, and screw it down. You may have to pull the wood to make these panels fit.

Finally, take the tail and slide it into the slot in the rear top panel until it touches the base. The wings are still square, so now is a good time to cut a curve onto the rear edges with a saber saw if you want to—remember that there is a beam set back from this edge, so make sure that any removal of wood will not cut into this beam.

below *An exploded view of the Plane.*

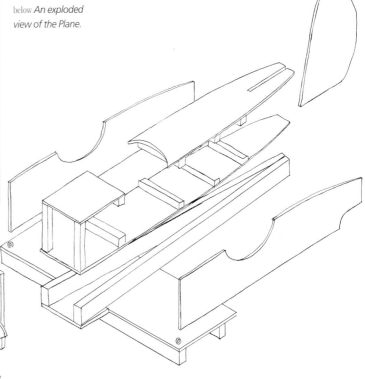

Do exactly the same for the other side panel, making sure that you keep it aligned with the one you have already positioned. Next, get the remaining named strips and fit them directly above their partners and the marks that they were measured from, between the two side panels. Make sure that they are ⅜ inch (the thickness of the top board) below the top edge of the side panel and screw through the side panels into the strips to secure them.

Take the front top panel and rest it on strip A up against the nose panel. Fasten it with screws through the side panel

1. *Adding the propeller.*

Because the structure is open to the elements and water can collect inside the fuselage, drill a few small holes in the floor (without damaging any fastenings) to allow for drainage.

PAINTING AND DECORATING

It is important to paint the tree house to protect the wood of the structure. Pay special attention to the structural beams and platform surfaces, and don't forget the underside. It is common when painting aircraft to paint everything below a midline white or sky blue, and everything above a bolder color.

FINAL DETAILS

The joy of flying is in being alone with the elements, but every pilot needs the right equipment: a flying helmet and goggles, a bomber jacket, and, of course, a flamboyant scarf. As for the passengers, they will appreciate some in-flight food and perhaps, if things get hairy, a parachute and a life raft.

FINISHING OFF

The interior of the Plane can be completed with the addition of two seats. They only need to be simple benches so they can be made by cutting two pieces of board that span between the two side panels and screwing it to them with wood strips. Don't forget that the interior of the fuselage is a great place to play, so don't block the entrance to it with the seats. Although it is not strictly accurate, the addition of a steering wheel gives a real sense of being the pilot and is much more satisfying and simple to attach than a joystick. Simply cut a circle from board or use an old car steering wheel and bolt it to the upper cross strip A. If that wood strip is not substantial enough, screw a block onto the underside of the front top panel.

One essential part is missing on the outside of the Plane: the propeller. Cut the propeller shape and two wooden washers from a piece of board and drill a hole through the center of them both. Then attach them to the center of the nose panel using a bolt that is not done up too tightly. The engine of the Plane can be represented by a series of pipe bends that have been pushed into holes cut in the side panels on either side of the Plane. If you prefer, you could make an engine cylinder block that sits behind the propeller by cutting it from board.

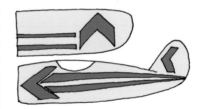

left *Some decorating ideas for your Plane.*

TREE HOUSES:
CUTTING PLANS

Cutting Plans

This section contains all the cutting plans for the various platforms and tree house variations described in the text. The cutting plans for each different type of platform and each structure variation are shown separately. This should make it easier for you to mix and match different platforms and structures as you like. When you build your tree house, you will need both a platform cutting plan and a structure cutting plan.

All cutting plans will fit on standard 4 x 8-foot board proportions. If your tree house works with these platform dimensions, all you need to do is transfer the plans to the appropriate number of boards and cut them out. If you want to work to a larger scale, you will have to scale up the plans accordingly, and possibly even rearrange the components to make better use of the wood that you intend to use. If you want to make a significantly larger tree house than those shown, we suggest that you consider adding additional components of your own design that will accommodate the longer spans and added complexity of a bigger, heavier structure.

To help make these plans useful for all sizes of tree house, we have used a basic grid along with alphabetic characters that indicate where a particular dimension is shared. So, a line marked "x" on one component will be the same dimension as any other line marked "x" in the same section. Capital letters are used to indicate component names, which are then described in the key.

Each standard board is represented as a grid. This grid is then subdivided 6 x 6-inch squares. Using the grid, it is easy to mark up your board. First, transfer the grid itself onto the board. Then transfer the various working lines, using the grid to help you mark them accurately. All the lines to be cut are marked in black. Any curves that do not have radii specified can be transferred freehand by working out exactly where they cross the grid lines and copying this information across.

If a curve seems too difficult to copy, try subdividing the grid into smaller squares.

Many of the projects also require additional boards for cutting out regular rectangular, square, or circular pieces. The number and size of the additional boards required are listed above the key; if the shapes require cutting out from the board, the dimensions needed are listed in the project's materials list.

The thickness of the board is marked below each grid. If this board thickness needs to be cut into a board, for example, where a board is slotted into place, then it is marked as "bt" (board thickness). Dotted lines are used to indicate both the position of a wood strip's crucial edge and the place where the edge of another board meets the first board.

- **BLACK LINES: Lines to be cut.**
- **DIAGONAL LINES: The position of a wood strip or the edge of another board.**
- **CAPITAL LETTERS: References to the component names explained alongside.**
- **LOWER-CASE LETTERS: References to edges that are the same dimension as others marked with the same letter.**
- **BT: Board thickness to be removed.**
- **SHADED AREAS: Wood to be discarded.**

BASIC PLATFORM FOR SINGLE TREE (PAGE 44)

You will also require the plans for the structure and one ³/₄ inch x 4 x 8-foot board for the platform.

A = 4 small support triangles (curved for the Pirate Ship, straight for the Desert Island Lodge). Cut one curved secondary support, then use this as a template for the rest.
B = 2 triangular supports

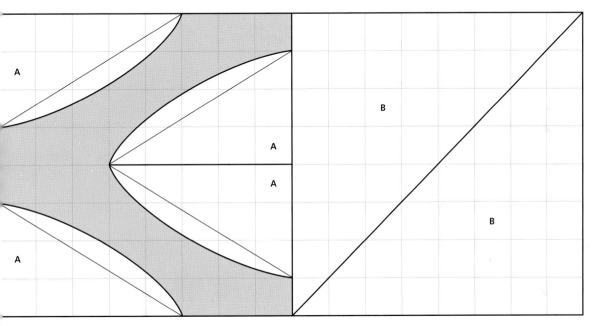

³/₄-inch board

DESERT ISLAND LODGE (PAGE 52)

There are no cutting plans, but you will need one ³/₄ inch x 4 x 8-foot board to cut out the walls and a second board the same size for the roof.

PIRATE SHIP (PAGE 56)

These are in addition to the plans for the basic platform.

A, B, C, F, G, H = curved supports
J = back wall
K = side walls

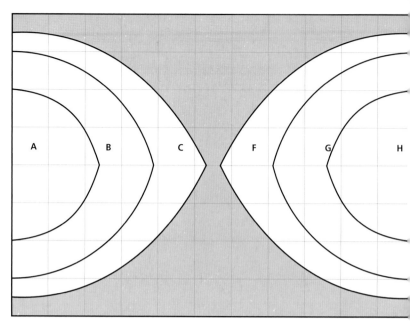

¾-inch board

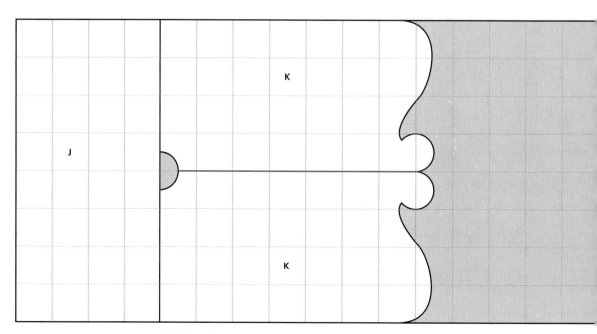

¾-inch board

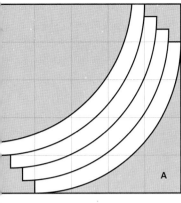

-inch board

PLATFORM VARIATION
FOR SINGLE TREE (PAGE 62)

You will also require the plans for the structure, one 3/4 inch x 4 x 4-foot board for the platform, and four 1/8 inch x 4 x 8-foot plywood boards to cut out the wall panel faces.

A = curved wall supports (24-inch radius)

WINDMILL (PAGE 66)

These are in addition to the plans for the platform variation. You will also need one 3/8 inch x 4 x 8-foot board to cut out the roof panels if you intend to use them.

A = front and rear walls, 1 of each required
B = side wall, 2 required

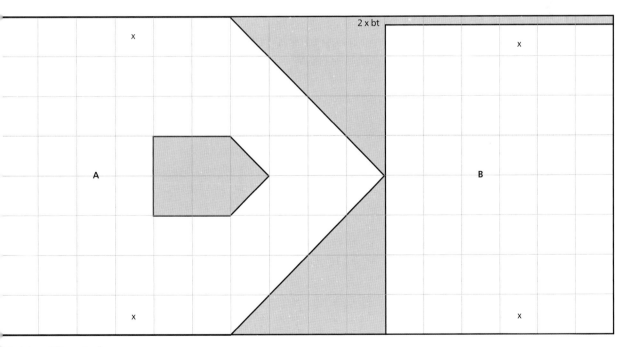

-inch board (2 required)

LIGHTHOUSE (PAGE 72)

These are in addition to the plans for the platform variation. You will also need one ¹/₈ inch x 4 x 8-foot plywood board to cut out four wall panel faces.

A = curved wall supports (24-inch radius)
B = roof
C = curved scraps for the roof
D, E = dome intersectors

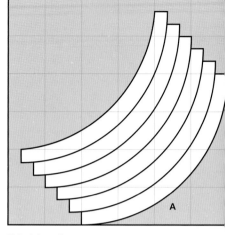

¾-inch board

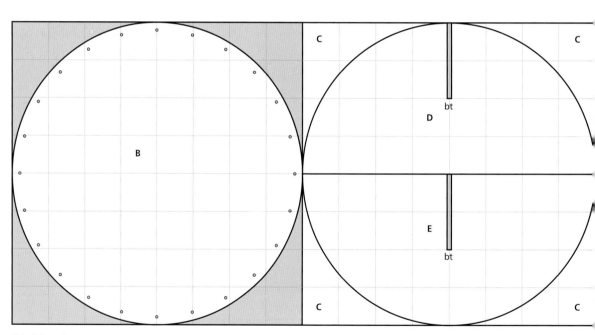

¾-inch board

MAGIC CARPET (PAGE 134)

You will also need one ¾ inch x 4 x 8-foot board for the platform. Both the straight and undulating carpets need both end covers (A). For the undulating carpet, cut the center curved support (B1) and curved side supports (C1); you will also need one ⅛ inch x 4 x 8-foot panel for the skin. For the straight carpet, you will only need to cut the straight fringed edges (C2).

A = end covers
B1 = center curved support: mark and cut this first, then use it as a template for all the other curves
C1 = curved side spports
C2 = fringed edges

= *where the pieces are joined to the platform*

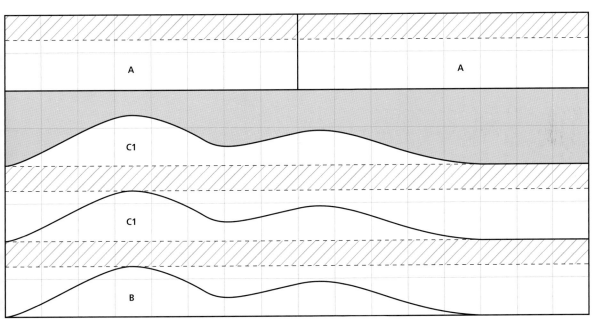

¾-inch board

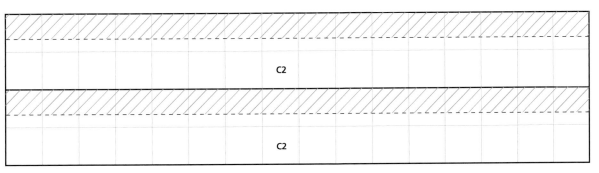

¾-inch board

SPOOKY HIDEOUT (PAGE 92)

These are in addition to the plans for the platform.

A, B = side walls
C = front walls
D = arch
E = back wall

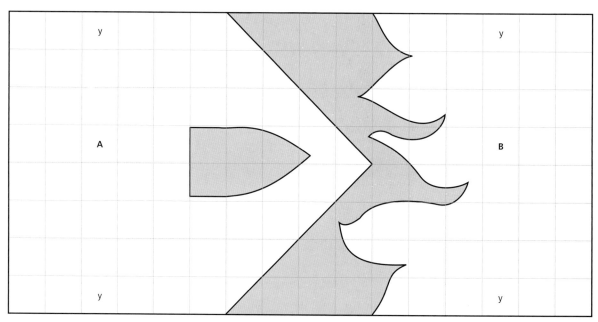

¾-inch board

BASIC PLATFORM FOR TREES WITH FORKED TRUNKS (PAGE 82)

There are no cutting plans, but you will need one ¾ inch x 4 x 8-foot board for the platform, and a second board the same size to cut out additional platform filler boards if needed.

THRONE (PAGE 86)

There are no cutting plans, but you will need one ¾ inch x 4 x 4-foot board for the platform.

BIRD'S NEST (PAGE 104)

There are no cutting plans, but you will need one ¾ inch x 4 x 8-foot board for the platform and the hoop.

BASIC PLATFORM FOR A PAIR OF TREES (PAGE 113)

There are no cutting plans, but you will need one ¾ inch x 4 x 8-foot board for the platform.

FORT (PAGE 120)

There are no cutting plans, but you will need two ¾ inch x 4 x 8-foot board for the platform and the hoop.

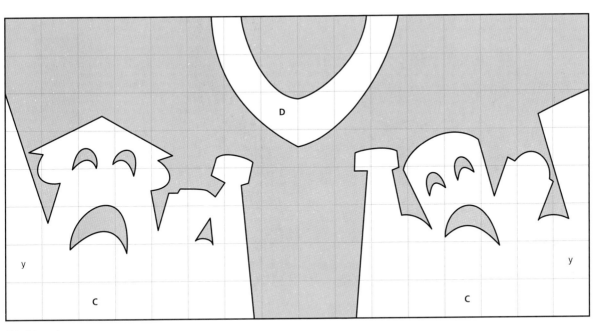

¾-inch board

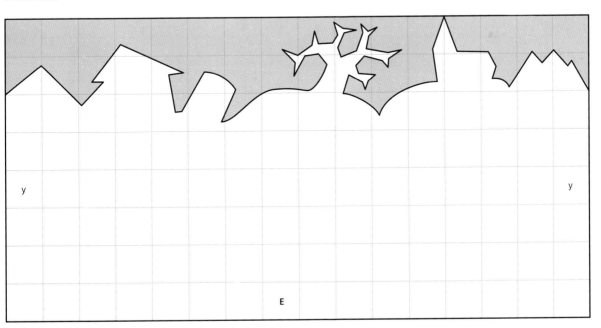

¾-inch board

153

ENCHANTED CASTLE (PAGE 98)

These plans are in addition to the plans for the platform. You will also need one $^1/_8$ inch x 4 x 8-foot plywood board to cut out four wall panel faces.

A = curved supports for upper platform walls (24-inch radius)
B = front walls
C = rear wall, 2 required. Use the scraps to secure them together
D = side walls, 2 required

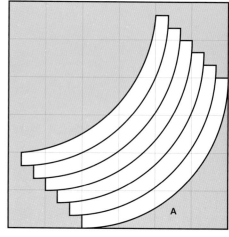

= *turret wood-strip positions*

¾-inch board

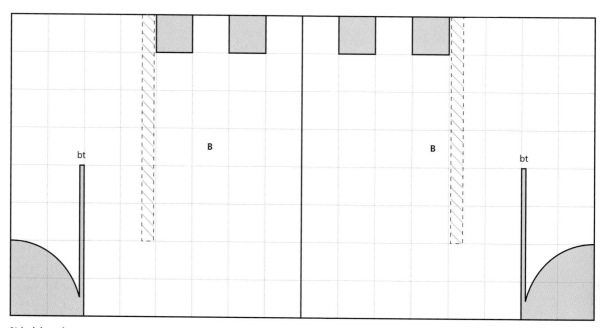

¾-inch board

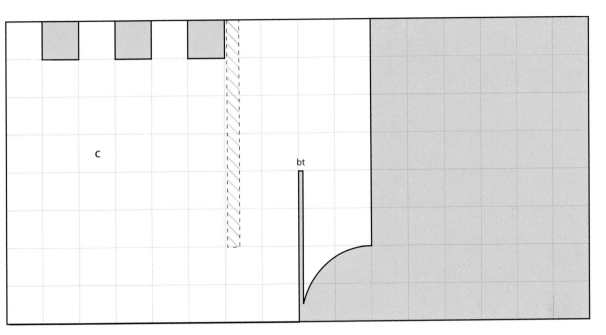

¾-inch board (2 required)

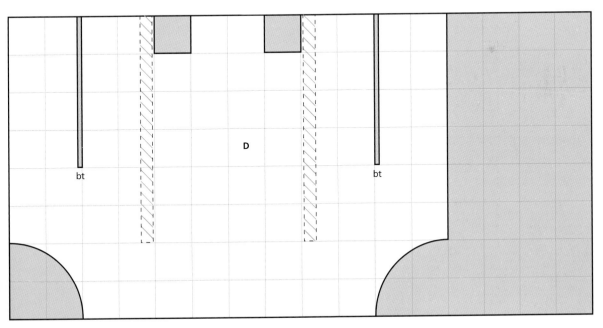

¾-inch board (2 required)

CAR (PAGE 126)

You will also need one ¾ inch x 4 foot x 8-foot board for the platform and one ⅛ inch x 4 foot x 5 foot plywood board to cut the curves for the front wing.

A = wheels, 4 required
B = raised hood panels, 2 required
C = front
D = bulkhead
E = seat backs
F = side panels
G = rear panel
H = seats
J = radiator support
K = radiator
L = trunk panel

 = where the sides are joined to the platform

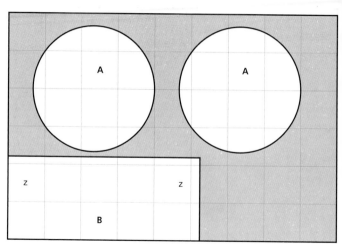

⅜-inch board

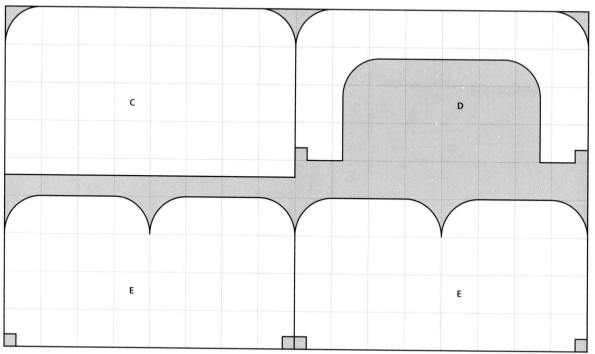

¾-inch board

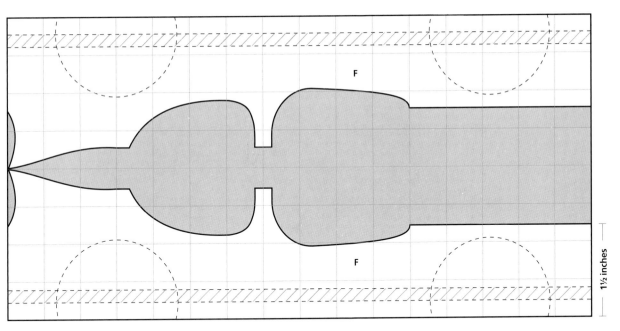

F

F

1½ inches

¾-inch board

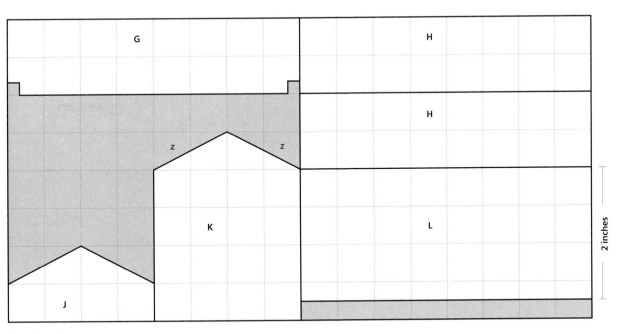

G

H

H

Z Z

K

L

J

2 inches

¾-inch board

PLANE (PAGE 138)

A = side panels
B, C = upper body panels (use D as a template to
draw them)
D = body nose panel
E = nose panel
F = propeller
G = tail
H = wing platform base
J = fuselage front panel platform base

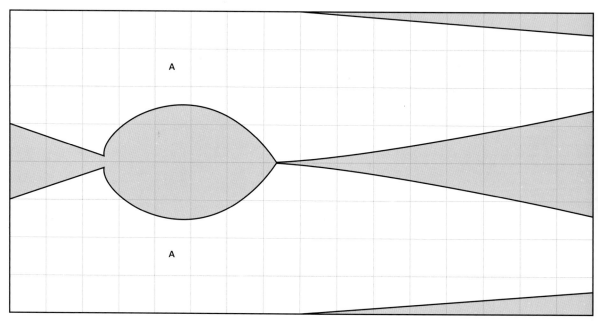

= *where the wood strips are attached*

A

A

⅜-inch board

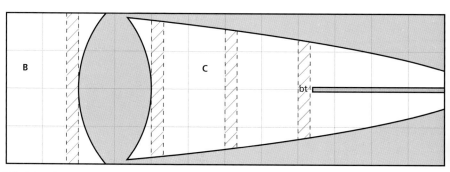

B   **C**   bt

⅜-inch board

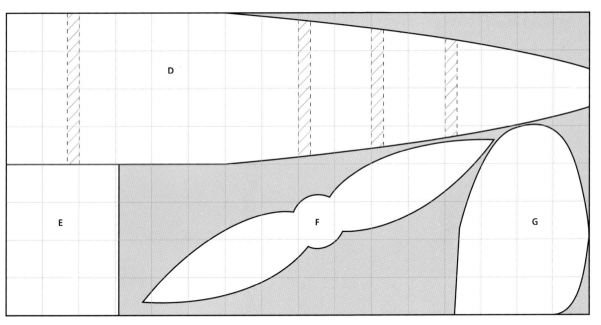

¾-inch board

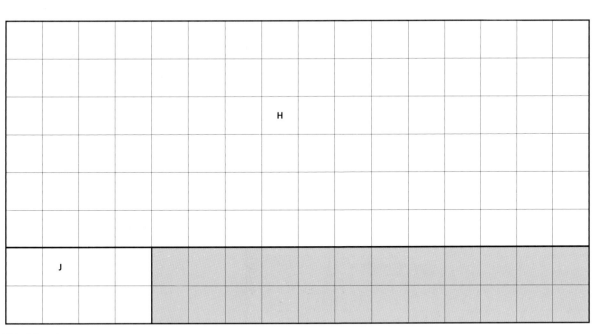

¾-inch board

Index